English 1

*Foundation Skills
for 11-14 year olds*

John Barber BA

Head of English,
Ward Freman School,
Buntingford

Denys Thompson MA

Charles Letts & Co Ltd
London, Edinburgh & New York

First published 1986
by Charles Letts & Co Ltd
Diary House, Borough Road, London SE1 1DW

Design: Ben Sands
Illustration: Edward Ripley, David Lock

© John Barber and Denys Thompson 1986

ISBN 0 85097 651 0

Printed in Great Britain by
Charles Letts (Scotland) Ltd

Acknowledgements

The authors and publishers are grateful for permission to quote from the following works:
Unit 1: *Little House in the Big Woods* by Laura Ingalls Wilder, published by Methuen Children's Books
Unit 2 *A Kind of Magic* by Mollie Harris, published by Chatto & Windus
Unit 3: *Passing of the Third Floor Buck* by Keith Waterhouse, published by Michael Joseph; *The Secret Diary of Adrian Mole, Aged 13¾* by Sue Townsend, published by Methuen London
Unit 4: The Iron Man by Ted Hughes, reprinted by permission of Faber and Faber Ltd
Unit 5: *The Lies of Boyo Butler* by Christopher Leach, reprinted by permission of Macmillan, London and Basingstoke
Unit 6: *Five Green Bottles* by Ray Jenkins, published by Macmillan Educational
Unit 7: The little sweep is adapted from the libretto of *Let's Make an Opera* (Eric Crozier) © 1949 by Hawkes & Son (London) Ltd, by permission of Boosey & Hawkes Music Publishers Ltd
Unit 8: *The African Child* by Camara Laye, published by Collins
Unit 9: *Jonathan Livingston Seagull* by Richard Bach, published by Turnstone Press Ltd, Denington Estate, Wellingborough, England
Unit 10: *First Four Minutes* by Sir Roger Bannister, published by Putnams, now in print with Dodd Mead
Unit 11: *Illustrated Guide to Britain*, copyright © 1974, Drive Publications Limited. Used with permission
Unit 13: *The Guardians* by John Christopher, published by Hamish Hamilton and Puffin Books
Unit 14: *A Child's Christmas in Wales* by Dylan Thomas, published by J M Dent
Unit 15: *The Day it Rained Forever* by Ray Bradbury, published by Rupert Hart-Davis Ltd
Unit 16: *The Middle-aged Man on the Flying Trapeze* by James Thurber © The Collection 1963 Hamish Hamilton from *Vintage Thurber*, published by Hamish Hamilton Ltd
Unit 17: *One Hundred Famous Haiku* edited by Daniel C. Buchanan, reproduced by permission of the Japan Publications Trading Co Ltd
Unit 18: *Short Stories* by Joyce Cary © Joyce Cary 1951, reproduced by permission of Curtis Brown Ltd, London
Unit 19: *Under Black Banner* by Geoffrey Trease, reprinted by permission of William Heinemann Ltd
Unit 20: *Something Borrowed* by Harry Secombe reprinted from *Argosy* Vol XXIX by permission of Harry Secombe

Unit 21: *Midnight is a Place* by Joan Aiken, published by Jonathan Cape Ltd
Unit 22: *The Listeners* by Walter de la Mare, reproduced by permission of the Literary Trustees of Walter de la Mare and The Society of Authors as their representative
Unit 23: Astronomy is reproduced by permission of Hamlyn Publishing, a division of the Hamlyn Publishing Group Ltd from *The Hamlyn Younger Children's Encyclopaedia*, Copyright 1972 The Hamlyn Publishing Group
Unit 24: *Pig in the Middle* by William Mayne, published by Hamish Hamilton Ltd
Unit 25: *The Hot Gates* by William Golding, reprinted by permission of Faber and Faber Ltd
Unit 27: *Kestrel for a Knave* by Barry Hines, published by Michael Joseph Ltd
Unit 28: *Once there was a king who promised he wouldn't cut anybody's head off* by Michael Rosen, published by André Deutsch
Unit 29: *The Silver Sword* by Ian Seraillier, published by Jonathan Cape Ltd
Unit 33: *Doll-Making: A Creative Approach* by Jean Ray Laury, reproduced by permission of Standard Scholarship
Unit 34: *No More School* by William Mayne, published by Penguin
Unit 36: *Ballet Shoes* by Noel Streatfeild, published by J M Dent & Sons Ltd
Unit 37: *Charlotte's Web* by E. B. White, published by Hamish Hamilton Ltd
Unit 38: *The Two Fiddlers* by George Mackay Brown, published by the Hogarth Press
Unit 39: *Friends and relatives* is reprinted from *A London Family between the Wars* by M. V. Hughes (1940) by permission of Oxford University Press
Unit 40: Cooking our food is reproduced by permission of Hamlyn publishing, a division of the Hamlyn Publishing Group Ltd from *The Hamlyn Younger Children's Encyclopaedia*, copyright 1972 The Hamlyn Publishing Group
Unit 41: *Earth is Room Enough* by Isaac Asimov, published by Granada Publishing Ltd
Unit 42: *Night Mail* by W. H. Auden, is reprinted by permission of Faber and Faber Ltd
Unit 43: *The Little House on the Prairie* by Laura Ingalls Wilder, published by Methuen Children's Books
Unit 44: *Fireweed* by Jill Paton Walsh, reprinted by permission of Macmillan, London and Basingstoke
Unit 45: The neighbours did not approve is reprinted from *Lark Rise to Candleford* by Flora Thompson (World's Classics Edition, 1954) by permission of Oxford University Press
Unit 46: *This Time Next Week* by Leslie Thomas, published by Constable Publishers
Unit 50: *Men and Gods* by Rex Warner, published by Granada Publishing Ltd

We are grateful to the following organizations and individuals for permitting us to reproduce photographs for which they hold the copyright: Catherine Ashmore: p 86; Barnaby's Picture Library: pp 8, 74, 88, 89; Jane and Colin Bord: p 44; Jim Brownbill: pp 38, 67; Camera Press: p 1; The Dean and Chapter of the Cathedral Church of Exeter: p 65; Mary Evans Picture Library: pp 27, 103; Fortean Picture Library: p 35; Sally and Richard Greenhill pp 15, 16, 17, 21, 37, 39, 97; Oliver Hunter: p 31; The Mansell Collection: pp 13, 18, 46, 47, 54, 59, 62, 72, 76, 79, 80, 85, 92, 110, 114; Peter Newark's Western Americana: pp 76, 100; Novosti Press Agency: p 108; Ronald Sheridan's Photo Library: p 79; Topham: pp 32, 73, 101, 102, 106, 112.

The photograph on p 59 is reproduced by courtesy of the Post Office and that on p 98 is Crown copyright. We are grateful to The Palitoy Company for supplying the Action Man shown in the photograph on p 81.

Preface

For parents in particular

You've bought this book to help your child with English. But the book is only part of the help parents can give. Good English comes from plenty of practice – in talking, listening, reading and writing.

So it's up to parents to talk to their children, listen to them, read to them, make suggestions for their writing, and enjoy what they've written.

Spelling and punctuation do matter; we want children to be accurate. *But* the content is more important. We want children to experiment with ideas, to be bold and adventurous, not to feel hemmed in by teacherly restrictions. Accuracy comes with reading and writing practice, and by encouraging young writers to correct their own work.

This is a book of doing, of action – not a book for copying out exercises. Action by parents is needed as well. How often one has heard something like this:

'I can't get my child to read . . . When I was young I read a lot.'
'Do you read much now?'
Silence . . .

English is exciting because it's about everything, every aspect of life . . . from filling in a driving licence application to writing a love letter . . . from explaining to the doctor precisely what is wrong to discussing which television programme to watch.

We have given many suggestions and activities in the book, but we are not expecting the young reader to do every single one; it is important to keep a sense of balance. There is no point in only writing stories or only following up the research topics.

The activities in this book, and in the second and third volumes, have taken into account recent official documents about the teaching of English, including *A Language for Life* (HMSO 1975), the tasks tested by the *Assessment of Performance Unit* set up in 1975, *Aspects of Secondary Education in England* (HMSO 1979), and *English from Five to Sixteen* (HMSO 1984).

4

Contents

Introduction

When you've been to a party that you've specially enjoyed, you probably want to talk about it. It's natural to talk; it helps us to keep alive something of our enjoyment.

The good bits, in particular, become fixed in our memories. Almost certainly you won't have realized that you were 'doing English'. *Talking* is important, and developed a long, long time before writing. It is one of the four areas of English we will be encouraging in this book and in the two volumes that follow.

Listening, another of the four areas, goes hand-in-hand with talking. After all, if you talk to someone you expect him to listen to you, and it's only right for you to listen when someone else does the talking. We tell you more about this in Unit 39, *Friends and relatives.* Apart from conversation, you need to listen carefully to instructions and in lessons.

Reading and *writing* complete our four areas of English. We hope that you will enjoy the pieces we have chosen and be tempted to read as many as you can of the books we recommend. Getting 'hooked on books' will give you hours and hours of pleasure, and gradually filling your book shelves with books is like increasing your number of

Melvyn Bragg – writer and broadcaster

friends. Books make good friends – they can't answer back!

Melvyn Bragg, who is a novelist apart from being a television presenter and producer, has said how exciting he finds *writing*. He remembers vividly writing his first short story. He hadn't sat down with the intention of writing a story, but he found himself starting a story and he was completely taken up by it. In fact, he doesn't even know how long he spent writing because he found it so absorbing. This is a case of getting 'hooked on writing'. And what a cheap and satisfying hobby writing can be; all you need is some paper and a pen or pencil. There can't be many cheaper hobbies.

Why bother with English? First, as we hope you have already gathered, we think it's exciting and we would like you to do so too. Secondly, the better you are at English the better you will become at most of your other subjects, and that's a pretty good reason, isn't it? Thirdly, and this stems from the last reason, much importance is attached to how good you are at English, not just while you are at school, but after you have left. The firmer you build the foundations now, the easier will the future become.

English is a subject that all schools take seriously, but unfortunately the number of lessons has to be limited. This book will give you that extra practice that will help you improve and will explain the skills (spelling, punctuation, style, and so on) you may be unsure about.

What each unit contains

We begin each unit with a piece from a short story, novel, article, play, or poem. Sometimes we have written an introductory sentence or two to help to set the scene. We offer a wide range of topics (what happened when a man came across a bear in his way; a seagull who rebels; Japanese poetry; how our words came about; tadpoles in wellington boots), and we hope you will enjoy reading them. There are bound to be some that appeal more than others, of course.

We have then written a

Comment

for you to read after the main piece. You will find more information about the book or the author, and we have tried to draw your attention to aspects we consider important. In some cases, having read the Comment, you will probably find it worthwhile to re-read the piece to which it applies.

Most of your time will be spent on the

Activities

which we have tried to make as varied and interesting for you as possible. We suggest listening, talking, reading and writing activities. But please don't feel that you have to work through *every* activity. You will be able to write stories and poems, make lists and tables, question friends and relations, record conversations, research in libraries and museums, curl up in a corner with a book. In some of the activities we ask you questions without indicating what we expect you to do with your answers. Take the second activity of Unit 2, for example:

    – What has been your experience of the suddenness of crazes? Is there one particular change-over you remember well? Some crazes are, of course, seasonal; conkers, for example.

You should *think* about crazes that you have known, not just those mentioned in the article (the Rubik cube might be a recent example). As you think, you can jot down your answers in your notebook. If there is a particular change-over you remember well you could write an account of the craze and the way in which the change-over to the next craze occurred. Did someone arrive at school with the new craze? Was a television programme responsible? You could write the activity as a diary entry: the day before, the day the new craze started, the following day. You could write a story about a boy or girl who started a craze and became suddenly popular as a result. In approaching such an activity, please think of possible ways of treating it. Part of the art of English is to look out for possibilities.

    Each unit finishes with

Nuts and bolts

which gives you hints and skills that you will find useful in improving the technical accuracy of your English. The emphasis, as our name for the section suggests, is on practical English.

    There is no answer section in this book because the activities can have many possible responses.

And the few questions that have a definite answer have sufficient clues for you to know if you are right.

What you need

Where do you write your notes and stories and poems? We recommend that you have the following, though it is really a matter of personal choice:

(**a**) a *notebook*
▶ for writing a first draft (or rough copy) which you will work on and improve before writing a fair copy,
▶ for jotting down notes from encyclopaedias in libraries,
▶ for noting questions you want to ask, etc.
In short, a multi-purpose notebook that can be taken around conveniently.

(**b**) a *folder* or *binder,* together with a pad of paper (both lined and plain)
▶ for your finished activities.

(**c**) a *dictionary* is an essential guide to have and *use* while working through the book.

(**d**) If you come across any poems or short extracts in the course of your reading that you particularly enjoy, write them out neatly in a *stiff-covered exercise book*.

(**e**) We suggest that, if you have become enthusiastic about a topic, you might like to have a separate *folder* just for that topic and carry out many more activities than we have given. (We mention this in the Comment for Unit 23, *Astronomy*.)

(**f**) A *cassette recorder* would be useful for some activities, but you can make good use of the book without one.

Handwriting

Good, legible handwriting is an asset both in school and in later life. If your handwriting is slovenly and difficult to read, now is the time to do something about it. There are various styles, but they all have several points in common:
▶ they are legible,
▶ the letters are even (a e o r, for example, are all the same height),
▶ if the letters slant at all at least they slant the same way. This is especially important with those letters that project below the line.

Presentation

Apart from taking care with handwriting, you should try to make the overall appearance of a page attractive. Leave a clear margin all round, training your eye to avoid a line ending in a jumbled group of letters crammed together.

How to use the table (pages 10 – 11)

On the left-hand side of the table you will see the titles of the units, while across the top of the pages you will see two sections: the first refers to listening and talking, reading and writing *Activities*; and the second indicates topics covered in *Nuts and bolts*. You can use the table as a quick reference guide. Greater detail is given in the Index on pages 117-120.

ACTIVITIES

We have numbered the activities here and in the index only for ease of reference. Had we done so in the units you might have felt they had to be answered in sequence and this is not the case.

		Thinking and noting	Imaginative writing	Personal experience	Lists/tables/charts	Diaries	Letters	Poetry	Script/dialogue	Conversation/oral work	Summaries	News item/headlines	Research	Dictionary work	Reading
1	The bear in the way			1	3, 5							2	6		7
2	Fun and games	1, 3	5	2						4					
3	Diaries		5			1, 3, 4							2		
4	The Iron Man	1, 4	2, 5									3			
5	Trouble with percentages			1, 2	3						4				5
6	That morning feeling!			1	3				2, 4	5					
7	The little sweep				6	2	5		1				8		7
8	The friendly snake			2						1, 3			4		5, 6
9	Practice makes perfect	2, 4	5	1				4		3			2	2	6, 7
10	First four minutes	1, 2	3, 4, 5		1										
11	The riddle of Loch Ness	4	2		3					4	5		1		
12	Letters	1, 6	2				3, 5								3
13	Rob's new school	1					2			3, 4					
14	Christmas	3, 4		1, 4								2			2, 5
15	Christmas in space	3	2		1						4		5		
16	Rex – the bull terrier	5, 6	1, 3	1									2		4
17	Haiku	2		4				1					3		
18	A special occasion	3		1, 2			4								
19	Lost on the hills	3, 7	1	5	6	4			2				6		
20	Something borrowed	4, 5	2	1						3					
21	A frightening experience	4, 5	2			1							3, 4	6	
22	The listeners	5, 6	2, 3, 4, 6							1			4, 5		
23	Astronomy	1, 4, 6								5			1, 2, 3, 7	8	6
24	Robert goes exploring		1, 3, 4, 5	3, 4						5				1	2
25	Billy	3, 5, 7	4		8	1			2				6		
26	English words	5										1	2, 3	4	
27	Fact and fiction	2, 4, 5		1, 3											6
28	Once there was a king . . .	4	2							5		1			5
29	Escape by canoe		1	2	5					5			3, 4		6
30	Pip and the convict	4, 5	1, 2, 3, 5												6
31	Adolf	1, 4	2, 3												5
32	The retired artist	3	1, 2	1, 2											4
33	Dolls	3	2	4						3			1, 5, 6		
34	Teachers for a month	3	1	2, 4							5				6
35	Life at Dotheboys Hall				2		1, 3		4				5		6
36	Pauline learns a lesson	1	3	1, 3, 4									2		5
37	Wilbur's new friends		3										4	1	2, 5
38	The king in rags	2, 4	1, 5	3											1
39	Friends and relatives	3, 4, 5, 6	3	2						1, 5, 6					
40	Cooking our food	1, 3, 4		2									5	6, 7	
41	The fun they had	1, 3					4	2	5						
42	Night Mail	1, 3	2		5					4					6
43	The tall Indian		4	3									1	2	5
44	A look at my head		3	4		6	1	5	2						
45	The neighbours did not approve	3, 4, 6		1, 2	5										
46	This time next week	1, 4	2, 3			2								5	
47	Children may be wiser	1, 2, 3, 5	4												6
48	The thrill of the circus	1	2			4							3, 5		6
49	Friends with the station master	1, 3	2	2		4									5
50	Pegasus – the winged horse	3	2, 3						4	5			5		1

NUTS AND BOLTS

Paragraphs	Sentences	Parts of speech	Punctuation	full-stops	commas	quotation marks	question marks	exclamation marks	hyphens	apostrophes	Capital letters	Spelling	additions to front	additions to end	plurals	families	I before E, etc.	Note-making	Summaries	Writing directions	Play scripts	Talking and writing	Conversation skills	Slanting style appropriate to audience	Similes
																						•			
																				•					
		•																							
•																									
		•																							
																					•	•			
		•																							
		•																							
			•																						
•																									
																			•						
												•													
	•																								
				•																					
						•																			
														•											
														•											
		•																							
		•																							•
					•																				
								•																	
•																									
												•													
												•													
															•										
										•															
									•																
	•																								
•																									
																		•							
									•																
																		•							
																•									
													•												
														•											
														•											
					•																				
																							•		
•																									
						•																			
										•															
												•													
																								•	
										•															
																			•						
																	•								
																		•							
																		•							
											•														

Unit 1

The bear in the way

Laura Ingalls Wilder lived a hard, but happy, life in a log cabin in America. This is an episode involving her father's return through the snowy woods, after he had been to the town to sell furs. Here he tells Laura and her sister what happened:

There were still six miles to walk, and I came along as fast as I could. The night grew darker and darker, and I wished for my gun, because I knew that some of the bears had come out of their winter dens. I had seen their tracks when I went to town in the morning.

Bears are hungry and cross at this time of year; you know they have been sleeping in their dens all winter long with nothing to eat, and that makes them thin and angry when they wake up. I did not want to meet one.

I hurried along as quick as I could in the dark. By and by the stars gave a little light. It was still

black as pitch where the woods were thick, but in the open places I could see, dimly. I could see the snowy road ahead a little way, and I could see the dark woods standing all around me. I was glad when I came into an open place where the stars gave me this faint light.

All the time I was watching, as well as I could, for bears. I was listening for the sounds they make when they go carelessly through the bushes.

Then I came again into an open place, and there, right in the middle of the road, I saw a big, black bear.

He was standing up on his hind legs, looking at me. I could see his eyes shine. I could see his pig-snout. I could even see one of his claws, in the starlight.

My scalp prickled, and my hair stood straight up. I stopped in my tracks, and stood still. The bear did not move. There he stood, looking at me.

I knew it would do no good to try to go around him. He would follow me into the dark woods, where he could see better than I could. I did not want to fight a winter-starved bear in the dark. Oh, how I wished for my gun!

I had to pass that bear, to get home. I thought that if I could scare him, he might get out of the road and let me go by. So I took a deep breath, and suddenly I shouted with all my might and ran at him, waving my arms.

He didn't move.

I did not run very far towards him, I tell you! I stopped and looked at him, and he stood looking at me. Then I shouted again. There he stood. I kept on shouting and waving my arms, but he did not budge.

Well, it would do me no good to run away. There were other bears in the woods. I might meet one any time. I might as well deal with this one as with another. Besides, I was coming home to Ma and you girls. I would never get here, if I ran away from everything in the woods that scared me.

So at last I looked around, and I got a good big club, a solid, heavy branch that had been broken from a tree by the weight of snow in the winter.

I lifted it up in my hands, and I ran straight at that bear. I swung my club as hard as I could and brought it down, bang! on his head.

And there he still stood, for he was nothing but a big, black, burned stump!

I had passed it on my way to town that morning. It wasn't a bear at all. I only thought it was a bear, because I had been thinking all the time about bears and being afraid I'd meet one. There I had been yelling, and dancing, and waving my arms, all by myself in the Big Woods, trying to scare a stump!

Little House in the Big Woods:
Laura Ingalls Wilder

Trapper's cabin
with bear pelts,
Alaska

Comment

Mr Wilder must have been very relieved when
he realized his mistake, though he wasn't yet
home and there could have been other bears
around. This episode is just one of many in which
the members of the family have to contend with
wild animals or severe weather conditions. Each
day had its own proper work to do in the home:

**Wash on Monday,
Iron on Tuesday,
Mend on Wednesday,
Churn on Thursday,
Clean on Friday,
Bake on Saturday,
Rest on Sunday.**

and there is a considerable amount to do; Laura's
father has to make all the furniture – after he has
built the house, of course!

Activities

– Can you remember an occasion when you were
very frightened, possibly in the dark, but which
had a happy conclusion? Write it down as a story
to be read aloud. You will make the fear come
over effectively if you describe the event simply
and without exaggeration.

– Imagine you have interviewed Mr Wilder about
the incident for the local Big Woods newspaper.
Make up a headline to attract the reader's
attention.

– Living with your family in an isolated region a
long way from neighbours, let alone a town or
village, what would you miss most? Make a short
list.

– Sketch out a ground plan for a log cabin.

– If you had to make all your own furniture, which
items would you make and in which order? (We
will assume you have the basic tools and
knowledge!)

– The Big Woods of the book's title refer to the
Wisconsin Woods in the state of Wisconsin in the
USA. Look up Wisconsin in an atlas and an
encyclopaedia, and make some notes for your
folder. How much of the state is still forest?

– This extract comes from Chapter 6, entitled *Two
Big Bears*. Find a copy of the book and read the
early part of the chapter in which Laura's sister
and mother push and slap what they think, in the
darkness, is their cow.

Nuts and bolts

Talking and writing

Read some of the story again, but this time aloud.
The words are written down just as Laura's father
spoke them, telling the girls his story. You can
imagine him sitting in front of the fire talking.
Most of us like to talk about what happens to us,
particularly if we have had an exciting or a
dangerous time. Talking is natural and gives us an
important starting-point for when we want to write.
Before you write, compose each sentence in your
mind and say it to yourself to see whether it is
going to sound right. Listen to the words in your
head and, when they flow effectively, that is when
they don't sound jerky, write them down. The
advantage of the written word is that you can keep
changing it. So, when you have finished a piece of
writing, read it through – aloud, if possible – to see
how it sounds. Make any alterations, if necessary.

– Look back at what you wrote for the first activity
in this unit. Does it flow when read aloud? Is it
effective?

Unit 2

Fun and games

There was no special time to start certain games. For weeks we all might be skipping madly, then one day someone would come to school with a bag of marbles or a whip and top, and suddenly all the other children did the same.

Probably many of the games had been handed down from earlier generations – ring games and ball games with singing and rhymes to accompany them. Some needed more than one child to play them, but it was nothing to see a small solitary figure, pigtailed and pinafored, bouncing a ball against a wall while counting, reciting, chanting or singing. The idea was to keep the ball in play through an ever-changing, intricate sequence of movements. The first dozen times it was simply thrown against the wall and caught, then bounced under the right leg, then under the left leg and finally bounced onto the wall again while the player spun round and caught it in midair.

Skipping was often done by solitary children. Our mother disliked the skipping craze because we wore out so much boot leather, but skip we would. Some of the children possessed proper ropes with nicely shaped wooden handles all painted red and blue. Poorer children had to be contented with any old bit of thick string they could get hold of. Skipping games usually started with a slowly spoken jingle. 'Salt, mustard, vinegar, pepper,' we would chant, then speed up the rope to finish with an exultant 'one hundred'.

As we progressed we could skip backwards – at least the rope was twirled backwards – or with the arms across the chest. And if you could jump in the air while the rope was twirled twice under your feet then you were really happy.

Whips and tops were most popular in the spring when the roads began to be dry and clean from mud and muck. You could buy a top for a ha'penny. There were different sorts, and we had a special name for each: carrot, granny, window breaker or spinny jinny. They were usually made of plain white wood but we would crayon the tops so that when they spun round they looked quite pretty.

The shortage of string for the whips presented problems. Who could afford to buy string? If we could get one of the older boys or girls who worked in the blanket mills at Witney to bring us a bit of 'mill bonding', a thickish, strong white string only used in the mills, then we were well away.

There was an art in keeping a top going by just thrashing it with a whip. The trouble with the 'window breakers' – sleek, slim tops they were – was the fact that they flew in the air as you whacked them, and if your aim was bad they often smashed straight through somebody's front window. Then there was hell to pay – at least the offender's parents were expected to buy new window glass. In the meantime the precious top and whip were flung on the fire.

Hoops was another game that was hard on boot leather. Some of the boys had large iron hoops which they skilfully steered for miles and miles with an iron hook. Girls, if they were lucky, had smaller wooden ones which they tapped gently with a stick – mostly we used old bicycle wheels and had just as much fun.

Marbles was a summer craze, a slower, quieter game, and if you had a penny you could buy twenty chalk marbles. A tally, which was the one you scattered the smaller ones with, usually cost a farthing and was often made of clear glass with bright multi-coloured wavy threads in. If you were lucky enough to find an empty lemonade bottle that had been thrown away, a sharp crack on a stone broke the bottle and released a super glass tally for nothing. Boys *and* girls played the game, but it was really considered more of a boy's game. The marbles were carried around in flannel bags secured tightly at the top with a thread of tape.

During the dry weather we girls played hopscotch – we would mark out the 'beds' with a bit of chalk. Sometimes the 'bed' would be six large squares joined together and in each square a number was written. The art of the game was to slide a small, flattish stone from one square to the next. This was done by hopping on one foot and gently kicking the stone along with the other so that it landed on the number. If the stone slid too far or landed on a line, then the player had to start again. The winner was the one who could complete the game without any faults.

There was little or no traffic on the roads and so we played games on the way to school. Six or seven of us would link arms – right across the narrow road we would stretch – singing, and before we knew where we were we'd walked the mile and a half, and were boiling into the bargain.

The most popular game for boys was 'Fox and Hounds'. On clear frosty winter evenings they would run for miles and miles. The lad chosen for the fox had to be a pretty good runner. He would dash off into the night and a little later the hounds would follow, shouting as they ran, 'Come out wherever you are, the dogs are on your tracks'. Often, after hours of chasing and running, the 'dogs' failed to catch their man and the game would be continued the next night, until the fox was caught.

A Kind of Magic: Mollie Harris

Unit 2 continued

Comment

The author, one of seven children, lived in an Oxfordshire village near Witney, a town famous for the production of blankets. Here, she writes of the enjoyment and absorption that she and her contemporaries experienced from the various games they played earlier this century.

One factor in particular was important for that community where there wasn't much money: the games played were either free or at least were fairly cheap. Ingenuity to improvize, using old bicycle wheels or bits of string, for example, had a part to play.

Another interesting feature is the suddenness with which the games changed. It just needed one person to begin a different game and the new craze started.

Activities

– How many of these games have you played? If you have played several, it would support what the author says in the second paragraph about games being handed down through the generations.

– What has been your experience of the suddenness of crazes? Is there one particular change-over you remember well? Some crazes are, of course, seasonal; conkers, for example.

– What games or crazes have there been during your schooldays – not necessarily those described in this unit? How many of them have involved very little expenditure? Are the best games free?

– Question your parents about the games they remember from their schooldays.

– Continue a story beginning:

It would never have happened if I had left the marbles where they were.

Nuts and bolts

Writing directions

Re-read Mollie Harris's directions for playing hopscotch. How clear do you find them? Did you know the game already? Is it different from the way you know? In writing directions there are some points to bear in mind.

First, it is important to give the exact *sequence* of the action. If the author had begun, 'The art of the game was to slide a small, flattish stone from one square to the next', we could quite rightly have said, 'Squares? What squares?' No, we are told, first, about marking out the six large squares with chalk.

Secondly, *jargon* or technical words must be kept to the minimum, though they can serve as a useful form of shorthand. Hopscotch is played on a 'bed', and the author quickly defines what she means.

Thirdly, *precise* words are necessary in order to avoid any possible confusion. Are there any words or phrases in the hopscotch directions that are not precise?

– Choose one of the games you have enjoyed playing most (now or when you were younger) and write clear directions for playing the game. Ask a friend to follow your directions exactly to see how good they are.

Unit 3

Diaries

Keith Waterhouse:

Monday 1 March, *St David's Day. Got up. Went to school. Came home. Had fish fingers. Went to bed. Started to count up to a billion but only got up to 7,643 for the reason that, my Father made me stop. He said that if he had to come up to my bedroom once more, that he would strangle me. This man is dangerous.*

Tuesday 2 March, *Got up. Had breakfast. Got ticked off by my Father for holding my breath. People should not get ticked off for holding your breath, for the reason that, it is a free country. Therefore I hate my Father. He thinks he is somebody but he is nobody. Also he have hair coming out of the end of his nose.*

Wednesday 3 March, *Ember Day. I am going to get my Father. He has been asking for it and now he is going to get it. Just because I was sucking bread. He go purple and bangs the table. If he was Run Over I would be glad. He look like a Jelly and also is Smelly.*

Thursday 4 March, *moon's first quarter 3.01 am. Got up. Went to school. Watched telly. Left roller skate at top of stairs, but it did not work. This only works in comics such as Whizzer and Chips etc., therefore, comics are stupid. They, the people you are trying to get, do not step on the roller skate and go ker-bam-bam-bam-bam-bam-kkkklunk-splat-aaargh. Instead of this, they just pick up the roller skate and say (This house getting more like a pig-sty every day). He is Potty and also Grotty.*

Friday 5 March *Today I said I was going to John's house but I did not, I went to the Pet Shop to buy a poisonous snake, but they did not have one. The copper-head, the Rattlesnake, the cobra and the Mamba are among the poisonous snakes to be found in the world. The man in the Pet Shop just laughed and tried to sell me a hamster. I am going to get him after I have got my Father.*

Dorothy Wordsworth

Dorothy Wordsworth:

1 March 1798 *We rose early. A thick fog obscured the distant prospect entirely, but the shapes of the nearer trees and the dome of the wood dimly seen and dilated. It cleared away between ten and eleven. The shapes of the mist, slowly moving along, exquisitely beautiful; passing over the sheep they almost seemed to have more of life than those quiet creatures. The unseen birds singing in the mist.*

23 May 1800 *Ironing till tea time. So heavy a rain that I could not go for letters.*

1 June 1800 *I heard a noise as a child paddling without shoes. I looked up and saw a lamb close to me. It approached nearer and nearer as if to examine me and stood a long time. I did not move. At last it ran past me and went bleating along the pathway seeming to be seeking its mother.*

Sue Townsend:

Tuesday January 6th *Epiphany. New Moon. The dog is in trouble!*

It knocked a meter-reader off his bike and messed all the cards up. So now we will all end up in court I expect. A policeman said we must keep the dog under control and asked how long it had been lame. My mother said it wasn't lame, and examined it. There was a tiny model pirate trapped in its left front paw.

The dog was pleased when my mother took the pirate out and jumped up the policeman's tunic with its muddy paws. My mother fetched a cloth from the kitchen but it had strawberry jam on it where I had wiped the knife, so the tunic was worse than ever. The policeman went then. I'm sure he swore. I could report him for that.

I will look up 'Epiphany' in my new dictionary.

Monday January 19th *The dog is back at the vet's. It has got concrete stuck on its paws. No wonder it was making such a row on the stairs last night. Pandora smiled at me in school dinner today, but I was choking on a piece of gristle so I couldn't smile back. Just my luck!*

Aubrey Herbert:

March 7 *. . . a horrible day. Five hours in a sandstorm. Kiazim's horse kept falling. The sand was frightfully painful to the eyes and yellow as a London fog. K. and I were separated for five minutes and the fear of being lost came upon us both . . . The dens for sleeping were nauseous. My head and feet touched either side of the room, and the floor was greasy.*

March 10 *Sixteen hrs march, the hottest day we have had . . . No water . . . Nearly drank from a green stinking puddle, but refrained. . . .*

Samuel Pepys:

1 January 1662 *Waking this morning out of my sleep on a sudden, I did with my elbow hit my wife a great blow over her face and nose, which waked her with pain – at which I was sorry. And to sleep again.*

6 January 1663 *Myself somewhat vexed at my wife's neglect in leaving of her scarf and waistcoat in the coach today that brought us from Westminster, though I confess she did give them to me to look after – yet it was her fault not to see that I did take them out of the coach.*

Comment

Many people keep diaries. For some, diaries help them to remember events dating back over months or years; for others, diaries make them more aware of their day-to-day lives.

The first entries, taken from *Passing of the Third Floor Buck* by Keith Waterhouse, and the third, from *The Secret Diary of Adrian Mole Aged 13¾* by Sue Townsend, are fiction. Although made up, they probably seem closer in style to the entries we imagine you would write. Keith Waterhouse's character wants to get his own back on his father, though we feel he does not really mean it. The writer has made mistakes of grammar and punctuation on purpose. Can you think why he does so?

The second diarist, Dorothy Wordsworth, in her entry for 23 May shows that one domestic activity at least – ironing – hasn't changed in nearly two hundred years!

Aubrey Herbert's entries record some experiences of a journey he made early this century from Baghdad to Damascus, while the entries from Samuel Pepys's famous diary give a fair impression of the sort of husband he was.

Activities

– If you do not keep a diary, try doing so for a week. You can keep a record of the main events of the day, including your progress in tackling the units in this book. It might provide interesting or exciting reading for a year's time. A character in one of Oscar Wilde's plays comments: 'I never travel without my diary. One should always have something sensational to read in the train.' Though we must point out that the character 'added to the truth' in her diary!
– Adrian Mole is going to look up 'Epiphany' in his new dictionary. What does he find? And what is an 'Ember Day' (Keith Waterhouse: Wednesday 3 March)?
– Write Mrs Pepys's diary entries for the two events described here by her husband.
– Imagine a diary entry for one of your teachers for the first day of a new term.
– You are rummaging around at home when you come across an old diary belonging to another member of your family. There is no one indoors, so you decide to be nosy. What secrets do you find?

Nuts and bolts

Nouns

When a teacher reads your work, he or she may make comments like: 'You need a verb somewhere' or 'You don't want a question mark'. *Verb* and *question mark* are technical terms invented to describe words and punctuation marks according to the work they do.

In the paragraph just above the first four nouns are: teacher, work, comments, verb. A *noun* names something; it comes from the Latin word *nomen* which means 'name'. Here are some nouns used in the unit: school, bedroom, stairs, snake, fog, policeman.
– Look at the last paragraph of Dorothy Wordsworth's Journal and, leaving out the date, find six nouns.

Unit 4

The Iron Man

The Iron Man lives on metal, and scares all the farmers by eating up their tractors. Despite his enormous size – his head is as big as a bedroom – they succeed in trapping him and then burying him in an enormous pit. However, he escapes; and then one of the farmer's sons, the boy Hogarth, has a bright idea. The farmers agree, and acting on Hogarth's plan they lead the giant to a large scrap-metal dump, telling him he can eat all he wants to:

At first, the farmers would not hear of it, least of all his own father. But at last they agreed. Yes, they would give Hogarth's idea a trial. And if it failed, they would call in the Army.

After spending a night and a day eating all the barbed wire for miles around, as well as the hinges he tore off gates and the tin cans he found in ditches, and three new tractors and a car and a lorry, the Iron Man was resting in a clump of elm trees. There he stood, leaning among the huge branches, almost hidden by the dense leaves, his eyes glowing a soft blue.

The farmers came near, along a lane, in cars so that they could make a quick getaway if things went wrong. They stopped fifty yards from the clump of elm trees. He really was a monster. This was the first time most of them had had a good look at him. His chest was as big as a cattle truck. His arms were like cranes, and he was getting rusty, probably from eating all the old barbed wire.

Now Hogarth walked up towards the Iron Man. 'Hello,' he shouted, and stopped, 'Hello, Mr Iron Man.'

The Iron Man made no move. His eyes did not change.

Then Hogarth picked up a rusty old horseshoe, and knocked it against a stone: Clonk, Clonk, Clonk!

At once, the Iron Man's eyes turned darker blue. Then purple. Then red. And finally white, like a car headlamps. It was the only sign he gave of having heard.

'Mr Iron Man,' shouted Hogarth. 'We've got all the iron you want, all the food you want, and you can have it all for nothing, if only you'll stop eating up all the farms.'

The Iron Man stood up straight. Slowly he turned, till he was looking directly at Hogarth.

'We're sorry we trapped and buried you,' shouted the little boy. 'We promise we'll not deceive you again. Follow us and you can have all the metal you want. Brass too, aluminium too. And lots of old chrome. Follow us.'

The Iron Man pushed aside the boughs and came into the lane. Hogarth joined the farmers. Slowly they drove back down the lane, and slowly, with all his cogs humming, the Iron Man stepped after them.

They led through the villages. Half the people came out to stare, half ran to shut themselves inside bedrooms and kitchens. Nobody could believe their eyes when they saw the Iron Man marching behind the farmers.

At last they came to the town, and there was a great scrap-metal yard. Everything was there, old cars by the hundred, old trucks, old railway engines, old stoves, old refrigerators, old springs, bedsteads, bicycles, girders, gates, pans – all the scrap iron of the region was piled up there, rusting away.

'There,' cried Hogarth. 'Eat all you can.'

The Iron Man gazed, and his eyes turned red. He kneeled down in the yard, he stretched out on one elbow. He picked up a greasy black stove and chewed it like a toffee. There were delicious crumbs of chrome on it. He followed that with a double-decker bedstead and the brass knobs made his eyes crackle with joy. Never before had the Iron Man eaten such delicacies. As he lay there, a

big truck turned into the yard and unloaded a pile of rusty chain. The Iron Man lifted a handful and let it dangle into his mouth – better than any spaghetti.

So there they left him. It was an Iron Man's heaven. The farmers went back to their farms. Hogarth visited the Iron Man every few days. Now the Iron Man's eyes were constantly a happy blue. He was no longer rusty. His body gleamed blue, like a gun barrel. And he ate, ate, ate, ate – endlessly.

The Iron Man: Ted Hughes

Comment

Termites can destroy wooden buildings and locusts consume every green thing for miles around, and there is no way of living with such enemies. But at present it is difficult to imagine anything that could digest metal, so you might say that this is not a good example of science fiction. Moreover in most science fiction a giant on the scale of the Iron Man would almost certainly be hostile in a way that Ted Hughes's Man is not. He is really a very amiable creature, bears no malice for the way he has been treated, and makes himself useful in our throwaway age, when there is rather too much waste lying about.

We notice two special points about the story. First, the adults are hopeless at finding a practical solution – their deception did not work – and it is a ten-year-old who supplies the sensible answer. Secondly, his solution is a peaceful one, and both sides benefit from it. Some authors would have been tempted to lay on a battle between the Iron Man and the Army. Perhaps there is a lesson here for the governments of the world.

Activities

– Can the Iron Man understand human speech? Has he any feelings? How do we know? Make a note of your replies.
– Invent some later events in the life of the Iron Man.
– Write up the events described above very briefly as a news item for radio.
– Think of some ways in which an automatic man could be useful now. He need not be as big as the Iron Man.
– You are the only human in a world of machines. Describe an event.

Nuts and bolts

Paragraphs

If you look at the pages of a book, you will see that the solid blocks of print are divided up into paragraphs. These are shown by indenting the first line of each paragraph, so that it starts a little way from the margin; these indentations are like notches or broken teeth. Sometimes in modern printing, as in this book for example, the first paragraph of a piece is not indented.

The aim of paragraphing is to make the material easier to take in, and to give the reader a break.
– In our unit the last two paragraphs begin 'The Iron Man . . .' and 'So there . . .' How do the second and third paragraphs begin?

Unit 5

Trouble with percentages

My first year there was terrible. The second wasn't all that good, either: but the first was murder. Landing up in a forest of fourth and fifth formers, giants all, with recently broken voices filling the air with foghorns, was like being born again into a very cold landscape. We clustered like visiting peasants near the gate, waiting for the whistle to say that we were doomed – and then it went, and they had us.

Those great echoing halls with the sounds of feet and teachers shouting commands: a different classroom for each subject, a different face, a different personality to get used to. Art saved me; and then English. I didn't mind those islands in a roaring sea. It was maths that killed me, day after day.

The teacher was large and red-faced, and had a moustache that looked as if a squirrel had gone to sleep under his nose. He had huge hands and he wore the same blue suit all the time I knew him. His voice was amazing in its range: it could whisper and wheedle and sing, and finally bellow. His eyes were like searchlights: they swivelled in his head, and he missed nothing – lighting up every mistake you made. He would bear down on you, waving your exercise book, slashed with corrections. As he did that last period, that Tuesday.

He stood over me (that ever-present smell of old pipe tobacco) and rammed his finger at a total.

'What is that?' he said.

'What, sir?'

'That, boy! *That*! How did you get an answer like that?'

The room was very quiet. Outside, the rest of the free world went about its business: a car changed gear in the road; a dog barked, untied, somewhere.

'Isn't it right, sir?'

'*Right*? Don't come the the old soldier with me, Butler. You know it's not right. Where's the *percentage*, boy? Look at the book. What does it say?'

'Give the answer as a percentage, sir.'

'Right. Stop that sniggering, Miller. *As a percentage*.' He tapped me hard on the head with an iron finger. 'Is there anything there, Butler? Does anything move under this thatch?'

'Yes, sir.'

'I doubt it, Butler. I doubt it. Now, when do I see you again? Third period tomorrow. I want to see that whole section done correctly. Do you hear me? If it isn't done correctly, I'll have to resort to other methods.' The iron finger tapped again. 'You know what I mean?'

'Yes, sir.'

'I shall make a special note, Butler. Third period tomorrow: *Butler's book*.' He closed the fat dog-eared diary, snapped home the elastic band. 'There's the bell. Off you go. Tomorrow, Butler. Third period.'

'Yes, sir.'

I walked home with Miller.

'He's got it in for you,' he said. 'He likes picking on you.'

'He knows I've got a more superior intellect,' I said. 'He knows I can take him, any time.'

'Not at maths.'

'At anything.'

'Wonder where he lives.'

'In a cave,' I said. 'He flaps home and hangs upside-down all night. Little red eyes in the dark, never closing.'

'Thinking up new problems,' said Miller, spoiling the picture. 'Double art, though, tomorrow.'

'In the afternoon,' I said. 'In the afternoon.'

'You'll be all right. That superior intellect.' He laughed. '*As a percentage*. Didn't you see that?'

'I'm not a mathematician,' I said. 'My world doesn't include algebra or geometry or decimal points. Or percentages. He can do his worst.'

'I've seen his worst,' said Miller. 'A big red five-fingered hand on someone's backside.'

'Who was that?' I said.

'Day you were away. He pasted Watson. Limped all the way home, he did: Watson.'

'You're a friend,' I said. 'A real pal. Thank you, and goodnight.'

'You doing anything special tonight?' he said. 'We could go up the club.'

'I'm having dinner with the Secretary for Education,' I said.

'Cheers,' said Miller, and crossed the road near the library.

The Lies of Boyo Butler: Christopher Leach

Comment

Poor Boyo Butler has a rough time with his maths, and his relationship with the maths teacher isn't too close! The description of the teacher, as seen through Boyo's eyes, is like a caricature: the moustache, blue suit, voice, searchlight eyes, smell

of old tobacco. If Boyo had been good at maths, would his description have been different? He might perhaps have viewed the teacher's red face as jolly and friendly.

The book isn't solely concerned with Boyo's maths. As the title indicates, Boyo has a 'lively imagination'. He imagines the maths teacher as a bat living in a cave, and he tells Miller he is dining with the Secretary for Education. These comments, and the comment about his 'superior intellect', are his way of coping with the unpleasant situation; he has been made to look a fool in front of the group and he wants to impress Miller by light-heartedly showing that he doesn't care.

set at school – perhaps percentages! Can you think of a particular problem which troubled you but which now causes you no difficulty? Try to pin-point exactly where the problem lay and write down some words of explanation, as if you were giving help and advice to a friend.
– You are Boyo's maths teacher. Write his maths report for the term.
– Find out what adventures happen to Boyo. Does he heroically save men from drowning, as he would like his mother to believe? Alan Ayckbourn has written a play about a boy who, in some respects, is similar to Boyo. It is called *Ernie's Incredible Illucinations*.

Activities

– Write about what you imagine happened 'Third period tomorrow'.
– In drawing a cartoon an artist picks out certain features. A caricature, a word we used in the Comment, is really a cartoon in words. Choose someone you know (it doesn't have to be a teacher!) and write a caricature by dwelling on two or three details. Take trouble to get just the right details. Or, draw a cartoon of Boyo's maths teacher, using the description from the third paragraph.
– Most of us have similar experiences to Boyo of not understanding some problem we have been

Nuts and bolts

Proper nouns

The names of people, places, months and so on belong to them specially; their names are their property, so they are called Proper Nouns. In our unit 'Boyo', 'Butler', 'Christoper' and 'Leach' are all proper nouns. Notice that they all begin with a capital letter.
– Find three more in the same unit.

Unit 6

That morning feeling!

An ordinary household. The play is set in the kitchen which is roomy and has access to the hall and living-room.

The time of the play is that period of rush between 8 o'clock and 8.45 a.m. on any weekday.

Gramp is reading the paper. Kevin is eating his toast. The radio is blaring cheery music. Mother is in the hall – calling upstairs.

MOTHER David! It's eight o'clock. Are you coming down or aren't you! David!

DAVID (*Upstairs*) All right!

MOTHER No 'all right' about it! Do you hear me!

DAVID (*Low*) Keep your hair on.

MOTHER (*Going up a couple of steps*) What did you say?

DAVID I'm combing my hair down.

MOTHER We'll have less of your lip, my lad. And I'm not calling you again. You'll be late. And tell that Maureen as well. (*Coming down the steps*) Talk about a house of the dead.

DAVID (*Hammering on a door*) Maureen!

MOTHER (*Shouting*) There's no need to shout!

DAVID (*Singing*) Maureen-O!

MOTHER Maureen, you'll be late! (*Pause*)

DAVID She's died in her sleep.

MOTHER I give up.

(*She comes back into the kitchen.*)
Nobody can get up in this house – you must get it from your father. If I slept half as much as you lot do there'd be nothing done –

KEVIN The world'd fall to bits –

MOTHER Kevin – get that telescope off the table –

KEVIN I'm looking at tomato cells.

GRAMP This paper's all creased!

MOTHER Don't moan, dad!

GRAMP It's like trying to read an elephant's kneecap!

MOTHER Why've you left that piece of bacon?

KEVIN It's all fat.

MOTHER You don't know what's good for you – it keeps out the cold –

KEVIN Why don't they make coats out of it then?

MOTHER That's enough. And turn that music down for heaven's sake – you can't even hear yourself think in a din like that.

KEVIN It's supposed to make you feel bright and breezy.

MOTHER You must be joking. Turn it off.

(*The radio is switched off.*)
Oh! A bit of peace at last!

GRAMP Never had bacon when I went to school. Just bread and jam and a four-mile walk.

KEVIN Aren't you glad you came to live with us then?

MOTHER Kevin, that's enough of that! There's a lot you youngsters today have to be thankful for and a full stomach's one of them.

GRAMP Just bread and jam and a five-mile walk.

KEVIN Four, you said.

GRAMP It might've been six if you count the hills. Where's my glasses! I can't read without my glasses.

KEVIN The cat's wearing them.

MOTHER Kevin! Oh I don't know. If it's not one it's the other.

GRAMP The words go up and down without them!

MOTHER (*Patiently*) Where did you have them last, dad?

GRAMP I had them just now.

MOTHER Are you sitting on them?

GRAMP Don't be daft – why should I sit on them?

MOTHER Stranger things have happened. Get up. Come on, get up.

(*Gramp gets up. He's been sitting on them.*)
There you are. What did I say?

GRAMP Who put them there, that's what I'd like to know!

KEVIN (*Low*) The cat.

MOTHER Do you want any more tea?

KEVIN No, thanks.

GRAMP Look, they're all twisted. You've got to have a head like a corkscrew to get them on now!

MOTHER (*Calling*) David! Maureen! I won't tell you again! It's ten past eight already! (*Pause*) What were you and David quarrelling about last night?

KEVIN Nothing.

MOTHER Nobody makes noise like that about nothing. What was it?

KEVIN Nothing.

(*He gets up.*)

MOTHER Where're you going?

KEVIN Get my books.

MOTHER You still haven't answered my question, young man!

KEVIN It was nothing – honest!

MOTHER Talk about blood from a stone. And take this telescope – I've only got one pair of hands.

(*Letters come through the front door.*)

There's the post.

(*A door slams upstairs.*)

DAVID I'll get them.

MOTHER Those doors!

KEVIN I'll get them.

MOTHER No, let David do it – it'll be one way of getting him downstairs.

(*David is cascading down stairs.*)

KEVIN It's always him.

Five Green Bottles: Ray Jenkins

Summary

The playwright opens with 'An ordinary household'. His intention is therefore to show a typical family scene. And what better time of day to indicate the various personalities in a family than a weekday morning, with all its tensions and frustrations! Mother tries to organize the family; she has to make sure everyone is out of bed and breakfasted before starting the day at work or school.

Both David and Kevin reply cheekily, and this provides some of the humour of the piece. The rest of the humour is supplied by Gramp, though he does not always realize it.

Activities

– Is a weekday morning in your family like this? What are you like in the mornings – bright and cheerful, grumpy? Write a paragraph or two about this morning.

– While she is out shopping that morning, Mother meets a friend of hers whose son is Kevin's friend at school. Make up a conversation and write it as a script. (See *Nuts and bolts* for how to set out a script.)

– How would you describe Kevin's character in this excerpt? List four or five words that could apply to him.

– Kevin and David arrive home from school. Write a short scene.

– With some friends, try making a recording of this excerpt. Don't forget to put in the sound effects.

Nuts and bolts

Play scripts

Whether they are written for stage, radio or television, scripts are set out differently from novels and short stories. As most of the words printed are spoken aloud, it would need lots of inverted commas. Just imagine the opening, set out as a story:

'David!' said mother. 'It's eight o'clock. Are you coming down or aren't you! David!'

'All right!' came David's reply from upstairs.

'No "all right" about it! Do you hear me!' said Mother.

'Keep your hair on,' mumbled David, so that his mother couldn't hear properly.

'What did you say?' said Mother, going up a couple of steps.

And so on.

This would be difficult for those acting the parts, so:

1 no speech punctuation is used, though all other punctuation marks are;

2 the characters' names are clearly marked at the side or in the margin, so that the actors can see quickly when to come in;

3 the playwright uses italics and/or brackets to indicate how the lines are to be said and what actions are to be made – (*Shouting*) (*He gets up.*)

– Check the activities above in which we asked you to write dialogue, to see if you have set the lines and directions out properly.

– Look at the previous unit, *Trouble with percentages*, and try writing some of the dialogue between Boyo and the maths teacher as a script.

Reminder

In *Nuts and bolts* in the first unit, *The bear in the way*, we stress the importance of composing each sentence in your mind, then saying it to see how it sounds. As a script is designed for saying aloud, it is advisable to test your lines in this way.

Unit 7

The little sweep

Gladys Parworthy is sitting by the fire in her drawing-room telling a true story to a group of children.

The story I am going to tell you took place in Suffolk long before I was born. It actually happened to my grandmother. Juliet was her name – Juliet Brook – and she lived at Iken Hall, a big Elizabethan house on the banks of the River Alde. It was a lonely house, miles from a village, surrounded by trees where herons nested and owls screamed at night.

When the story begins Juliet was fourteen. She had a brother and a younger sister. Their cousins were staying with them for the Christmas holidays. The holidays were coming to an end, and it was nearly time for the cousins to go home to Woodbridge, where they lived. They had brought their own nursery-maid to look after them and that was just as well, for all the children loved Rowan, but not one of them liked Miss Baggott. She was a crusty, cantankerous, overbearing old housekeeper with a sharp word always biting her tongue!

Country houses in those days – in eighteen hundred and nine, or ten – had big open hearths and winding brick chimneys. When they needed sweeping, little boys were sent up into the soot and the darkness to scrape them clean. Sam Sparrow was a sweep-boy like that. Only eight years old, poor child!

His father was a waggoner, and so dreadfully poor that there was nothing for it but selling little Sam to Black Bob the sweepmaster. Oh, he was a ruffian, Black Bob was! His son Clem was as cruel as his wicked father. Just imagine poor Sam's feelings when they took him to Iken Hall, stripped all the clothes off him and drove him up into the blackness of his first chimney.

He climbed and scraped, and then he climbed a bit higher and scraped again, choking with soot, and up he went, and up – till he found himself wedged in the neck of the flue so that he couldn't move up or down at all. He was frantic, as well he might have been. He shouted 'Help! Help! I'm stuck!' Luckily Juliet and the others heard him.

Black Bob had tied a long rope round his waist in case of accidents. They tugged on that and – Crash! – down he tumbled.

There they were – six young children in nice clean clothes, with a filthy little boy lying in the fireplace and sobbing as though his heart would break. All they could get out of him was 'Please don't send me up again!' Over and over again he said it.

Juliet and the others decided that they couldn't hand him over to the sweeps – nor to Miss Baggott – so they hid him. First they laid a trail of sooty footsteps to the window, to deceive the sweeps into thinking Sam had run away, and then they hid him in the toy-cupboard among their hoops and dolls for a whole day and a night!

Not only did they bath Sam and feed him and dress him in clean clothes, but they managed to smuggle him out of the house under Miss Baggott's very eyes!

It was time for the cousins to go back to Woodbridge. Sam went with them in the top of a trunk. They let him out as soon as they were clear of the house, and off they went down the high-road as merry as crickets, to the rattle and gallop of the horses' feet.

Juliet's uncle took pity on him and set him to work in the garden at Woodbridge. When my mother was a girl, old Samuel Sparrow had grown to be head-gardener. He used to give her apricots on her birthday.

Let's Make An Opera: Libretto by Eric Crozier

Comment

Gladys's story about the little sweep begins *Let's Make An Opera* by Benjamin Britten, who wrote the music, and Eric Crozier, who wrote the words. The first two acts are in the form of a play, and illustrate the preparation and rehearsal of 'The Little Sweep', an opera performed in Act Three. The characters discuss whether they should turn the story into a play or an opera. Gladys thinks it would be good as an opera: 'Opera is very like Shakespeare – it speaks in a magic language of its own and reveals all the wonderful and terrible and exciting things that lie beneath the surface of everyday life.' One of the other characters adds that many people quite wrongly 'think of opera in terms of outsize sopranos and swans going backwards'. They realize that there will be lots to do: writing and learning the words and music, building scenery, making properties and costumes, and plenty of rehearsing. But they decide it's going to be worthwhile.

Activities

– The story is simple and effective. If you had to write the script, where would you begin – in the sweepmaster's house, with Bob telling young Sam what to do; with Juliet and the family; with Miss Baggott opening the door to Sam and his master? Write the first scene in play form. See Unit 6 to remind yourself how to set it out.

– Write Juliet's diary for the two days of the story.

– Draw a plan of the stage for the main action. You will need to position a fireplace and chimney, a window, a toy-cupboard, and furniture.

– Design costumes for Miss Baggott and Black Bob.

– Imagine Sam is now in his eighties. You have heard about the incident when he was eight and you would like to write his biography (that is, the story of his life). Write a letter to him asking if it would be possible to interview him, giving him some reasons.

– Make a list of questions you would like to ask Sam concerning his one experience of being a sweep.

– There are various stories and poems about boy-sweeps. Try *The Water Babies* by Charles Kingsley, or two poems by William Blake, both of which are called 'The Chimney Sweeper'; one is in *Songs of Innocence* and one is in *Songs of Experience*. You should be able to find the poems fairly easily. Which poem do you prefer?

– Nobody, by law, can send a young boy of eight up a chimney to scrape away the soot. Try to find out how it became a law. You may need to ask a history teacher or a librarian which books to look at.

Nuts and bolts

Pronouns

These stand instead of nouns, and in this way save endless repetition. For example, the first paragraph of the story above would be very clumsy if all the time we had to use nouns instead of the pronouns: I, she, it.

– Find some pronouns in the last paragraph of the unit.

Unit 8

The friendly snake

Ever since the day I had been forbidden to play with snakes, I would run to my mother as soon as I saw one.

'There's a snake!' I would cry.

'What, another?' my mother would shout. And she would come running out to see what sort of a snake it was. If it was just a snake like any other snake – actually they were all quite different – she would beat it to death at once; and like all the women of our country she would work herself up into a frenzy, beating the snake to a pulp, whereas the men would content themselves with a single hard blow, neatly struck.

One day, however, I noticed a little black snake with a strikingly marked body that was proceeding leisurely in the direction of the workshop. I ran to warn my mother as usual. But as soon as my mother saw the black snake she said to me gravely:

'My son, this one must not be killed: he is not as other snakes, and he will not harm you; you must never interfere with him.'

Everyone in our compound knew that this snake must not be killed; excepting myself, and, I suppose, my little playmates, who were still just ignorant children.

'This snake,' my mother added, 'is your father's guiding spirit.'

I gazed dumbfounded at the little snake. He was proceeding calmly towards the workshop; he was moving gracefully, very sure of himself, and almost as if conscious of his immunity; his body, black and brilliant, glittered in the harsh light of the sun. When he reached the workshop, I noticed for the first time, cut out level with the ground, a small hole in the wall. The snake disappeared through this hole.

'Look,' said my mother, 'the serpent is going to pay your father a visit.'

Although I was familiar with the supernatural, this sight filled me with such astonishment that I was struck dumb. What business would a snake have with my father? And why this particular snake? No one had to kill him, because he was my father's guiding spirit! . . . But what exactly was a 'guiding spirit'? What were these guiding spirits that I encountered almost everywhere, forbidding one thing, commanding another to be done? I could not understand it all, though their presences were around me as I grew to manhood. There were good spirits, and there were evil spirits; and more evil than good ones, it seemed to me . . . I was absolutely baffled, but I did not ask my mother about it; I felt I would have to ask my father himself . . .

I began by questioning him in a roundabout manner and on every subject under the sun. Finally I asked:

'My father, what is that little snake that comes to visit you?'

'What snake do you mean?'

'Why, the little black snake that my mother forbids us to kill.'

'Ah!' he said.

He gazed at me for a long while. He seemed to be considering whether to answer or not. Perhaps he was thinking how old I was, perhaps he was wondering if it was not a little too soon to confide such a secret to a twelve-year-old boy. Then suddenly he made up his mind.

'That snake,' he said, 'is the guiding spirit of our race. Can you understand that?'

'Yes,' I answered, although I did not understand very well.

'That snake,' he went on, 'has always been with us; he has always made himself known to one of us.'

'How did he make himself known?' I asked.

'First of all, he made himself known in the semblance of a dream. He appeared to me several times in slumber, and he told me the day on which he would appear to me in reality; he gave me the precise time and place. But when I really saw him for the first time, I was filled with fear. I took him for a snake like any other snake, and I had to keep myself in control, or I would have tried to kill him. When he saw that I did not receive him kindly, he turned away. And there I stood, watching him depart, and wondering all the time if I should not simply kill him there and then; but a power greater than myself stayed my hand and prevented me from pursuing him. I stood watching him disappear . . .'

He was silent for a moment, then went on:

'The following night, I saw the snake again in my dream. "I came as I foretold," he said, "but thou didst not receive me kindly; nay, rather I did perceive that thou didst intend to receive me unkindly: I did read it in thine eyes. Wherefore dost thou reject me? I am the guiding spirit of thy race, and I make myself known to thee, as to the most worthy. Therefore cease to look with fear upon me, for behold I bring thee good fortune." After that, I received the serpent kindly when he made himself known to me a second time; I received him without fear, I received him with loving kindness, and he has brought me nothing but good.'

The African Child: Camara Laye

Comment

This comes from the story of his childhood and youth by a young West African, who was eventually sent to Paris to finish his education. His father was a goldsmith, who shaped into jewelry the gold brought to him by women. When the snake visited him, he would stroke it; and then the snake would curl up and watch him working at the anvil.

Incidentally if you come across a snake sunning itself in heath-land, do not kill it. It may be a slow-worm – which is not a snake at all, but a lizard – or a grass snake, which is completely harmless. Even an adder (yellow with a pattern of big black diamonds down its back), will attack only when frightened.

Activities

– We have left out a few lines of dialogue in which the boy questions his father about the snake. Invent the short conversation between the two.
– Describe a visit to the Reptile House at a zoo.
– Prepare a two-minute talk on 'Snakes'.
– Find out about making and running a vivarium.
– Find a copy of D. H. Lawrence's poem, *Snake*, and read it carefully, aloud, enjoying the subtle rhythms and sounds. (The poem appears in full in Volume 2.) Here is an extract to whet your appetite:

> *He reached down from a fissure in the*
> *   earth-wall in the gloom*
> *And trailed his yellow-brown slackness*
> *   soft-bellied down, over the edge of*
> *   the stone trough*
> *And rested his throat upon the stone bottom,*
> *And where the water had dripped from*
> *   the tap, in a small clearness,*
> *He sipped with his straight mouth,*
> *Softly drank through his straight gums,*
> *   into his slack long body,*
> *Silently.*

– Read Alan Wykes' *Snake Man* or one of Gerald Durrell's books about collecting animals.

Nuts and bolts

Verbs

These tell us about movement or action or the state people are in. For example, at the beginning of the unit the first six verbs are: had been forbidden, play, would run, saw, 's, cry. Note that the first verb is made up of three parts, the third of two; and that, here, 'is' dwindles to 's' and is tacked on to 'there'.
– Look at the extract from *Snake* in the Activities and find four different verbs there.

Unit 9

Practice makes perfect

Jonathan Livingston Seagull is no ordinary seagull; or is he?

It was morning, and the new sun sparkled gold across the ripples of a gentle sea.

A mile from shore a fishing boat chummed the water, and the word for Breakfast Flock flashed through the air, till a crowd of a thousand seagulls came to dodge and fight for bits of food. It was another busy day beginning.

But way off alone, out by himself beyond boat and shore, Jonathan Livingston Seagull was practising. A hundred feet in the sky he lowered his webbed feet, lifted his beak, and strained to hold a painful hard twisting curve through his wings.

The curve meant that he would fly slowly, and now he slowed until the wind was a whisper in his face, until the ocean stood still beneath him. He narrowed his eyes in fierce concentration, held his breath, forced one . . . single . . . more . . . inch . . . of . . . curve . . . Then his feathers ruffled, he stalled and fell.

Seagulls, as you know, never falter, never stall. To stall in the air is for them disgrace and it is dishonour.

But Jonathan Livingston Seagull, unashamed, stretching his wings again in that trembling hard curve – slowing, slowing, and stalling once more – was no ordinary bird.

Most gulls don't bother to learn more than the simplest facts of flight – how to get from shore to food and back again. For most gulls, it is not flying that matters, but eating. For this gull, though, it was not eating that mattered, but flight. More than anything else, Jonathan Livingston Seagull loved to fly.

This kind of thinking, he found, is not the way to make one's self popular with other birds. Even his parents were dismayed as Jonathan spent whole days alone, making hundreds of low-level glides, experimenting.

He didn't know why, for instance, but when he flew at altitudes less than half his wingspan above the water, he could stay in the air longer, with less effort. His glides ended not with the usual feet-down splash into the sea, but with a long flat wake as he touched the surface with his feet tightly streamlined against his body. When he began sliding in to feet-up landings on the beach, then pacing the length of his slide in the sand, his parents were very much dismayed indeed.

'Why, Jon, why?' his mother asked. 'Why is it so hard to be like the rest of the flock, Jon? Why can't you leave low flying to the pelicans, the albatross? Why don't you eat? Jon, you're bone and feathers!'

'I don't mind being bone and feathers, Mum. I just want to know what I can do in the air and what I can't, that's all. I just want to know.'

'See here, Jonathan,' said his father, not unkindly. 'Winter isn't far away. Boats will be few, and the surface fish will be swimming deep. If you must study, then study food, and how to get it. This flying business is all very well, but you can't eat a glide, you know. Don't forget that the reason you fly is to eat.'

Jonathan nodded obediently. For the next few days he tried to behave like the other gulls; he really tried, screeching and fighting with the flock around the piers and fishing boats, diving on scraps of fish and bread. But he couldn't make it work.

It's all so pointless, he thought, deliberately dropping a hard-won anchovy to a hungry old gull chasing him. I could be spending all this time learning to fly. There's so much to learn!

It wasn't long before Jonathan Gull was off by himself again, far out at sea, hungry, happy, learning.

The subject was speed, and in a week's practice he learned more about speed than the fastest gull alive.

From a thousand feet, flapping his wings as hard as he could, he pushed over into a blazing steep dive towards the waves, and learned why seagulls don't make blazing steep power-dives. In just six seconds he was moving seventy miles per hour, the speed at which one's wing goes unstable on the upstroke.

Time after time it happened. Careful as he was, working at the very peak of his ability, he lost control at high speed.

Climb to a thousand feet. Full power straight ahead first, then push over, flapping, to a vertical dive. Then, every time, his left wing stalled on an upstroke, he'd roll violently left, stall his right wing recovering, and flick like fire into a wild tumbling spin to the right.

He couldn't be careful enough on that upstroke. Ten times he tried, and all ten times, as he passed through seventy miles per hour, he burst into a churning mass of feathers, out of control, crashing down into the water.

The key, he thought at last, dripping wet, must be to hold the wings still at high speeds – to flap up to fifty and then hold the wings still.

From two thousand feet he tried again, rolling into his dive, beak straight down, wings full out and stable from the moment he passed fifty miles per hour. It took tremendous strength, but it worked. In ten seconds he had blurred through ninety miles per hour. Jonathan had set a world speed record for seagulls!

Jonathan Livingston Seagull: Richard Bach

Comment

This book is a good fable (that is, a story with a moral, often about animals) because it is very easy to see that it is as much about human beings as seagulls. In fact, the author gives the game away by dedicating the book 'To the real Jonathan Seagull, who lives within us all'.

What type of person/seagull is Jonathan? He is a determined individual who concentrates very hard on one thing, practising again and again after each failure until he succeeds. We think of him as so much more alive and interesting than the other seagulls.

After his parents have urged him to be 'normal' and to fit in, he vows he is going to try to be good; but it isn't long before he works out how to fly at 140 miles per hour. He eventually achieves an astonishing speed, almost double that!

Activities

– The conversation he has with his parents probably sounds familiar: 'Why is it . . .? Why can't you . . .? Why don't you . . .?' Think back to a similar occasion at home, and either write down what happened or use it as the basis of a short story.
– There are various sorts of seagulls in the British Isles. Look up in a bird book and make a list of the gulls found in the 'family'. Gulls are said to be 'gregarious'. Find out what this means. Does it account for the attitude of Jonathan's parents?
– Do you know anyone like Jonathan who practises hard – at a sport, perhaps, or a musical instrument? Ask about the amount of time and dedication needed. You will find most enthusiasts like to talk about their hobby.
– When you next see a gull write somes notes describing how it sits, flies, hovers, lands. Make some quick sketches to accompany your words. This might lead to your writing a poem. (Unit 17, *Haiku*, might give you some ideas.)
– Make up a fable of your own, involving two animals, perhaps a cat and a goldfish.
– Learn about Jonathan's further adventures; how he has to 'Stand to Centre for shame in the sight of your fellow gulls!' and is banished to a solitary life. But things change.
– Another book you might like to try is *Watership Down* by Richard Adams. This book is about rabbits, rather than gulls. Kenneth Allsop's book, *Nature Lit their Star*, is also recommended.

Nuts and bolts

Punctuation

This was invented to break up solid pages of reading matter into small, easily understood parts. In the earliest books, like the handwritten Bibles, there was no punctuation at all; the reader had to supply his own. In the Exeter Book (see Unit 26) it looks as if the monks who copied it have put in some stops. In this book we are dealing with the most important stops; the rest we are leaving till a later book.

In the paragraph we have just written there are nine punctuation marks.
– How many punctuation marks are there in the last paragraph of our extract? Read the paragraph aloud. Do you see how they help?

Unit 10

First four minutes

There was complete silence on the ground . . . a false start . . . I felt angry that precious moments during the lull in the wind might be slipping by. The gun fired a second time – Brasher went into the lead and I slipped in effortlessly behind him, feeling tremendously full of running. My legs seemed to meet no resistance at all, as if propelled by some unknown force.

We seemed to be going so slowly! Impatiently I shouted 'Faster!' But Brasher kept his head and did not change the pace. I went on worrying until I heard the first lap time, 57.5 sec. In the excitement my knowledge of pace had deserted me. Brasher could have run the first quarter in fifty-five seconds without my realizing it, because I felt so full of running, but I should have had to pay for it later. Instead, he had made success possible.

At one and a half laps I was still worrying about the pace. A voice shouting 'relax' penetrated to me above the noise of the crowd. I learned afterwards it was Stampfl's. Unconsciously I obeyed. If the speed was wrong it was too late to do anything about it, so why worry? I was relaxing so much that my mind seemed almost detached from my body. There was no strain.

I barely noticed the half-mile, passed in 1 min. 58 sec., nor when, round the next bend, Chataway went into the lead. At three-quarters of a mile the effort was still barely perceptible; the time was 3 min. 0.7 sec., and by now the crowd was roaring. Somehow I had to run that last lap in fifty-nine seconds. Chataway led round the next bend and then I pounced past him at the beginning of the back straight, three hundred yards from the finish.

I had a moment of mixed joy and anguish, when my mind took over. It raced well ahead of my body and drew my body compellingly forward. I felt that the moment of a lifetime had come. There was no pain, only a great unity of movement and aim. The world seemed to stand still, or did not exist. The only reality was the next two hundred yards of track under my feet. The tape meant finality – extinction perhaps.

I felt that at that moment it was my chance to do one thing supremely well. I drove on, impelled

Roger Bannister at the finish of the first sub-four-minute mile at the Iffley Road track

by a combination of fear and pride. The air I breathed filled me with the spirit of the track where I had run my first race. The noise in my ears was that of the faithful Oxford crowd. Their hope and encouragement gave me greater strength. I had now turned the last bend and there were only fifty yards more.

My body had long since exhausted all its energy, but it went on running all the same. The physical overdraft came only from greater will power. This was the crucial moment when my legs were strong enough to carry me over the last few yards as they could never have done in previous years. With five yards to go the tape seemed almost to recede. Would I ever reach it?

Those last few seconds seemed never-ending. The faint line of the finishing tape stood ahead as a haven of peace, after the struggle. The arms of the world were waiting to receive me if only I reached the tape without slackening my speed. If I faltered, there would be no arms to hold me and the world would be a cold, forbidding place, because I had been so close. I leapt at the tape like a man taking his last spring to save himself from the chasm that threatens to engulf him.

My effort was over and I collapsed almost unconscious, with an arm on either side of me. It was only then that real pain overtook me. I felt like an exploded flashlight with no will to live; I just went on existing in the most passive physical state without being quite unconscious. Blood surged from my muscles and seemed to fell me. It was as if all my limbs were caught in an ever-tightening vice. I knew that I had done it before I even heard the time. I was too close to have failed, unless my legs had played strange tricks at the finish by slowing me down and not telling my tiring brain that they had done so.

The stop-watches held the answer. The announcement came – 'Result of one mile . . . time 3 minutes' – the rest lost in the roar of excitement. I grabbed Brasher and Chataway, and together we scampered round the track in a burst of spontaneous joy. We had done it – the three of us!

We shared a place where no man had yet ventured – secure for all time, however fast men might run miles in the future. We had done it where we wanted, when we wanted, how we wanted, in our first attempt of the year. In the wonderful joy, the pain was forgotten and I wanted to prolong those precious moments of realization.

First Four Minutes: Roger Bannister

Comment

We live in an age of record-breaking. More knowledge of human beings and our surroundings, new machines and materials, all make this possible. The development of sports and games offers more opportunities. But there are not many accounts, like this one, which tell us exactly what it felt like at the time.

A great deal of record-breaking is the result of team-work. This attempt – to run a mile in under four minutes – succeeded because a number of people co-operated, such as Stampfl the coach, and Bannister's friends, Brasher and Chataway, who trained with him to act as pace-makers. Each of the two ran a lap at exactly the speed fixed by the coach as the right one; and as soon as each had done his lap, closely followed by Bannister, they dropped out, leaving him to run the last three hundred yards on his own.

Activities

– Bannister succeeded through team-work. How helpful did he find the crowd? Have you ever been helped by a friend standing at the side of a pitch or track, urging encouragement? Did it make a difference to you?
– What sort of record-breaking do you admire? Why does it appeal to you? Look in *The Guinness Book of Records*, readily available in school and public libraries, if you need some ideas. What records would you yourself like to break?
– Is there any journey you would like to make very slowly rather than very fast? Describe the journey as you imagine it.
– Imagine you get involved in a record-breaking attempt, and say what happens.
– 'The Great Race' – write a short story with this title. The race can be any kind of race.

Nuts and bolts

Paragraphs

The divisions into paragraphs are not just made 'any old how', at random. The breaks come when they are needed. In a story, for instance, the scene changes; time moves on; and events take a fresh turn. All these will require separate paragraphs. It is the same with writing about an experiment in a laboratory, or the different parts of a machine.

If you look at the second paragraph of our unit ('We seemed . . .') you will see that Bannister is describing only one stage of the race.
– Can you say what the next three paragraphs are about? (This is not difficult.)

Unit 11

The riddle of Loch Ness

Whatever it is that stirs in Loch Ness, it is no newcomer. An inscription on a 14th-century map of the loch tells vaguely but chillingly of 'waves without wind, fish without fins, islands that float'. The description has seldom been bettered by the hundreds of witnesses who have testified to the creature's existence.

'Monster' sightings are not limited to Loch Ness: Lochs Awe, Rannoch, Lomond and Morar have all been said to contain specimens. The Loch Ness Monster owes its greater fame to the opening of a main road along the north shore of the loch in 1933. Since then, distant views of 'four shining black humps', 'brownish-grey humps', 'a wave' that shoots across the loch at 20 mph, have kept visitors flocking to the loch.

People who have seen the phenomenon more closely say that it is 'slug-like' or 'eel-like', with a head resembling a seal's or a gigantic snail's, while the long neck is embellished with a horse's mane. Its length has been estimated at anything between 25ft and 70ft, and its skin texture is 'warty' and 'slimy'. Close observers too, particularly Mr George Spicer and his wife who saw it jerking across a lochside road in 1933, have declared it 'fearful' and 'an abomination'.

So far, the creature has presented itself only in tantalising glimpses. To believers it has been an unknown fish, a giant slug, and a plesiosaurus, which was (or is) a fish-eating dinosaur. Unbelievers are equally imaginative. They suggest that the 'monster' is really a mat of rotting vegetation propelling itself by released gases; waterfowl such as red-throated divers swimming in line ahead; a group of otters playing 'follow my leader'; even the remains of a First World War Zeppelin that appears periodically on the surface of the loch. In Gaelic folklore there is no mystery; the animal is an *Each Uisge*, one of the fearsome water-horses which haunt almost every sheet of dark water in the Highlands.

It is not surprising that such waters, cupped in savage hills, should produce legends. Loch Ness is part of the Great Glen, a geological fault that slashes across Scotland like a sword-cut. The loch itself is 24 miles long, about a mile broad and has an average depth of 400ft.

Loch Ness has one direct outlet to the sea, the shallow River Ness, and it is fed by eight rivers and innumerable streams, each of which pours the peaty soil of the hills into the loch. Consequently, the water is dark. Divers working with powerful arc lamps 50ft below the surface have been unable to see for more than 10ft around them. Legends of caves said to be the home of a colony of monsters have yet to be disproved; these are supposed to be situated beneath the rocky ruins of Urquhart Castle.

Stories of a 'beast' in Loch Ness date back at least to the 6th century. It is recorded in Adamnan's biography of St Columba that in AD 565 the saint prevented a River Ness water monster from eating a Pict. According to another legend, the beast towed St Columba's boat across the water, and was granted perpetual freedom of the loch.

Such benevolence does not sound like the normal behaviour of the Gaelic water-horses. Sometimes these would appear on the lochsides in the guise of milk-white Shetland ponies, bridled and saddled; and if a child attempted to ride one of them, it would carry him into the water.

Over the past 40 years, sightings have been claimed by more than 1000 people. Most of the sightings were in bright sunlight in conditions of flat calm, and several of the witnesses were trained observers – soldiers, doctors, seamen and waterbailiffs. Though many of the sightings were from a distance, witnesses have been convinced they were looking at a large animal, most of whose body was hidden beneath the water.

If it exists, it is most unlikely that the Loch Ness monster is a single animal. A prehistoric creature, living alone in Loch Ness, cut off from others of its kind, would have to be millions of years old. For the species to survive there must be quite a large colony; discrepancies in reported sizes could be accounted for by the presence of adults and young. The colony theory is also supported by nearly simultaneous sightings in different parts of the loch.

MISS GOODBODY'S SKETCH.

"MONSTER" BEING CAREFULLY OBSERVED BY MR. W.U. GOODBODY & HIS TWO DAUGHTERS FROM 11·45 A.M. TO 12·25 P.M. DECEMBER 30TH 1933, ABOUT 2½ MILES FROM FORT AUGUSTUS. DISTANCE VARIED BETWEEN 400 & 700 YARDS. (FROM DRAWINGS MADE UNDER THEIR SUPERVISION)

According to naturalists, the chances of the creature being a reptile are remote. Though Loch Ness never freezes, its temperature never rises above 6°C (42°F) and this would be too cold for any known species. Also, reptiles breathe air, and would have to surface more frequently than the monster appears to. Fish, too, would seem to be ruled out, if legends and accounts of the animal's shore-going activities this century are to be believed. This leaves the invertebrates, and certainly many of the descriptions would fit an enormous worm or slug. But there is no evidence that a backbone-less creature of such bulk has ever existed on this planet.

Though most zoologists deny the possibility that a large and unknown animal might be living in Loch Ness, it is remarkable that reports of creatures in other Scottish lochs, and in lakes in Ireland, Norway and British Columbia, should be so similar in detail. Meanwhile, the mystery continues; and it is perhaps more exciting than any final scientific solution.

AA Illustrated Guide to Britain

Loch Ness Monster Descriptions

Believers	*Unbelievers*

Comment

This article gives an account of the sightings of the Loch Ness Monster going back over many centuries; it's a long history. A tourist reference book has to interest a large number of readers from all walks of life – young, old, men, women. The writer must be careful to present opinions and evidence in a balanced way, particularly in a topic like this where there are 'believers' and 'unbelievers'. He or she acts like a referee, being fair to both sides.

Activities

– Find Loch Ness, and the other lochs mentioned in the second paragraph, on a map of Scotland.
– You are on holiday near Loch Ness. Having read the article you decide to spend a whole day by the side of the Loch hoping to have a glimpse of the monster. You come equipped with camera and binoculars. It is late afternoon, and you won't be able to wait much longer (someone's coming to pick you up), when there is a tremor on the surface of the lake. Write what happens.
– Make a list of the descriptions of the monster by believers and another list by the unbelievers. Set your lists out in columns:

– What are your views on the monster? Which theory seems to you to be the most likely? Look through the article to find the most convincing reasons for the monster's existence. Talk to your friends and see what they believe.
– You have a pen-friend to whom you normally send a postcard while you are on holiday. Space is limited on a postcard, but you decide to explain about the monster. You have only eighty words!

Nuts and bolts

Summaries

These are much used. Nearly everything in a newspaper is a summary of a longer version; and serial stories usually start with a summary of previous events.

The difference between notes and summaries is that the former tend to be scrappy and usually read by the person who made them; whereas summaries are meant for other people, so they must be fuller and easy to understand at once.

This is our attempt to summarize the first paragraph of our unit: 'For hundreds of years, people have seen something mysterious in Loch Ness'.
– Now you have a go at summarizing the second paragraph.

Unit 12

Letters

Everyone likes getting letters, and it may be that the older we grow the more we welcome them. The first letter we ever receive gives us the feeling that we really matter to someone outside the home.

The next step is when we form close relationships and exchange long letters at times of separation. At the same stage perhaps we fall in love for the first time, and eagerly await the letter which gives us a hint that our love is returned. As children grow up, letters between them and their parents become important; probably they matter more to the parents than to their sons and daughters. Usually, parents love their children more than their children love them; this may be sad, but it is one of the facts of life and only to be expected, because parents feel so much responsibility for their offspring's welfare, they get worried when they are separated and anxious to know that all is well. Perhaps this will come to mind if ever you have to live away from home; your parents will hope to hear from you, as much and often as possible. When we are young it is difficult to realize how much pleasure Mum and Dad get from our letters and how eagerly they are awaited. Other kinds of letters also mean a great deal both to sender and receiver, for example when a person has to leave home for some time owing to the demands of business or a job. Sometimes these letters are kept, and when, for example, they are written by a man or woman in wartime, they can be a truly valuable record. In such letters there is more of the truth about what war is really like than in histories and newspapers.

Collections of letters are a big branch of literature and are good history too because they tell us what people thought and felt about things. One example is the Paston Letters, written five hundred years ago. They bring home to us the lawlessness of the Middle Ages when a big householder in the country had to leave an armed guard on his house when he was away, or on his return he might find it taken over by a neighbouring lord. But letter-writing for everybody was not possible till 1840, when Sir Rowland Hill introduced the penny post and ordinary men and women took up correspondence in a big way.

Incidentally do you know anyone with a stamp collection? If so, ask to be shown the first stick-on stamp, the Penny Black. And you'll see from the collection that the penny post lasted till just on your grandparents' time. There were then 240 pennies in a pound, and you could send a postcard for a ha'penny.

However only about one in a million people thinks about publication when he writes letters,

and the letters won't be any the better for it. You are more likely to be concerned with letters to relatives, or when you are on holiday, or away from home, or someone is in hospital; and some people play chess by post or learn a language through a penfriend scheme. Others write an occasional letter to a newspaper; and newspapers do seem to welcome letters from young people, when they are short and to the point on a subject the writer knows something about. We recall a very good letter in a local newspaper from someone at school, about a plan to cut down a fine avenue of trees to make more room for cars.

There are two main kinds of letter. The first is informal and friendly, between people who know each other fairly well or very well – acquaintances, friends and relatives. The other is the formal or business type of letter, for example a request for a catalogue of things you are interested in; we are leaving that to another book. Everyone likes to have interesting well-written letters, and as

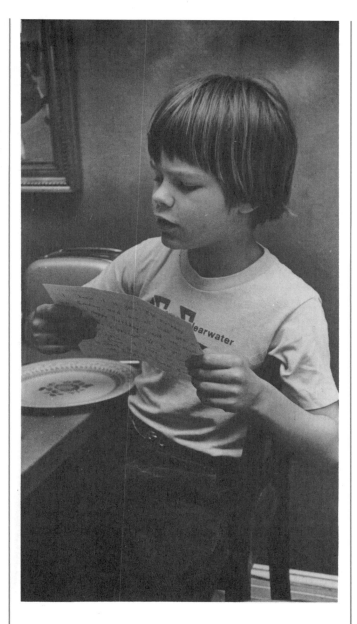

W. H. Auden wrote in 'Night Mail': 'Who can bear to feel himself forgotten?' The best way to get good letters is to write them. Someone from your form who has to stay in hospital will be delighted to get a letter full of news to relieve the long hours in bed – and a bundle of comics as well. Do not hesitate to include in such letters things that may not seem worth reporting at all; parents especially want to know everything.

When you write, always give your full address, with the number of the house and the post-code. The latter eases sorting and makes delivery accurate. A letter to someone outside the family (like a teacher) who is fairly well known will start with one of: 'Dear Mrs or Miss or Ms or Mr,' and will end 'Yours sincerely'. To a friend a common ending is 'Yours ever'; this is better than funny endings like 'Yours till hell freezes', which is fine at first, but gets boring. Within the family the usual ending is 'With love from . . .' or possibly 'Your loving daughter/son . . .'.

Comment

We have said enough to show the place that letters can occupy in our lives, especially when we are separated from home or friends. There will certainly come a time in your life when you will long for a letter, so it is worth remembering that even now there may possibly be someone who would be greatly cheered by an interesting letter from you. Obviously good letters take time and thought, like anything that is worth doing.

Activities

– Having read all that we have written above about correspondence, what do you think is the main point in writing family and friendly letters? Answer in one sentence, but write it down; this makes sure that you make up your mind.
– Describe the letter that you would most like to receive.
– Read the correspondence in any comic or magazine or newspaper; and if you feel strongly about any of the topics, write a reply or comment.
– Make a little picture of your house or something in the district, or an initial letter, and if possible make a lino-cut to print at the head of note-paper.
– In the Comment we suggest that there may be someone who would like a letter from you. This could be just the moment!
– If your parents get any official or business letters, ask to borrow some and compile rules for writing such letters.

Nuts and bolts

Spelling

Anyone who wants to can improve his or her spelling. There are several methods, but we believe ours is the best. We do not give lists of words for learning, because we think that the better plan is for you to make your own lists of words you want to remember.

Start your own list of difficult and interesting words by writing them down in a page at the end of your notebook (or in a separate notebook, if you wish). Cross them out as you become absolutely certain of them. If you have doubts about 'receive', write it down, but we hope that when you have taken in Unit 47 you will be able to cross it out.

Unit 13

Rob's new school

This piece comes from a science fiction tale of the future. Because Rob is an orphan he has to go to a boarding school:

For the first few days he was too confused to take in much beyond an impression of constant activity. The day was filled to overflowing. Broadcast alarms woke the dormitories at six-thirty and there was a scramble to wash and dress and reach the games area by seven. They were nearly a quarter of a mile from it. You had to run, in wet weather with a cape flapping round you. On arrival there was roll-call. Late-comers, if only by half a minute, were put on report and given extra gymnastics in the evening.

The half-hour of exercises in the morning was theoretically followed by half an hour's free time before breakfast at eight o'clock. But you quickly learned the importance of queuing in advance outside the dining-room because the food, apart from being poor and badly cooked, was never sufficient to go round. For those at the end of the queue the horrible lumpy porridge was further diluted with hot water, there was half a portion of reconstituted egg or half a rissole, and there might not even be a slice of bread. Senior boys pushed their way to the front at the last minute: juniors had no option but to stand in line.

Morning school was from eight forty-five till twelve-thirty, when there was a break for lunch and more queuing. In the afternoons they had games – gymnastics again in bad weather – until tea at half past four. Then there was evening school from five to seven, after which you were free until lights out at nine. Free, that is, if you had not been detailed for extra gym, or for one of the hundred jobs which prefects or other seniors required to have done. Rob went to bed exhausted each night and slept soundly on a lumpy three-section mattress. . . .

They went into class – History of Engineering. The master was a small neat grey-haired man who rattled through his talk quickly and perfunctorily. He was dealing with rocket propulsion, flashing slide after slide through the projector. He asked for questions in a way that did not invite response, but Rob said:

'It's not much used now, is it, sir?'

The master looked at him in some surprise. He said:

'Hardly at all . . . There are no really useful applications.'

'It was chiefly intended for interplanetary exploration, wasn't it, sir? Why was that given up? Men landed on the Moon, and probes reached Mars.'

The master paused before replying: 'It was stopped because it was pointless, Randall. Is it Randall? Millions of pounds were spent on utterly useless projects. We have different priorities now. Our aims are the happiness and well-being of mankind. We live in a saner, more ordered world than our fathers did. Now, if you have satisfied your vanity by interrupting, we will get on with the lesson. A much more useful invention, and one that is still used in an improved form, is the jet engine. The origin of this. . . '

Some of the other boys were looking at him in disgust. In his old school it had not been popular to ask questions. He realised it was probably going to be worse here.

He wondered if the world was really so much happier than in the past. No one starved, it was

true, and the only war was the far-away one in China. No one who stayed out of trouble had to fight in that if they did not want to. There were holovision and the Games, the Carnivals – all kinds of amusements. Riots, too, of course, but they were over quickly and mostly people could avoid them. Many seemed to enjoy them. What the master had said was probably right.

The Guardians: John Christopher

Comment

This comes from a story about a school of the next century. The author wrote his book as a warning to young people that they must free themselves from the kind of world that we seem to be drifting into. He tells us what this world will be like: everyone will follow the same pursuits – holovision, watching the Games and 'all kinds of amusements', with rioting as another popular entertainment. Rob's school prepares its pupils for their future by discouraging them from thinking for themselves.

Activities

– Your present school is probably a much happier place than Rob's. Jot down some of the differences; for instance, think what happens when people ask questions.
– Imagine yourself as a new pupil at Rob's school.

Write a letter to a younger brother or sister, giving your impressions at the end of the first week of term.
– If you were given the chance of questioning the head of Rob's school on television, what questions would you like to ask him? You could ask a friend to take part in a mock interview. Both of you would need some time to prepare.
– Question an adult (parent, grandparent, neighbour) about his or her early experiences at secondary school. What kind of things are remembered? You might like to tape the conversation. Compare experiences.

Nuts and bolts

Sentences

A sentence is a group of words that make sense. For example, the words 'from a science fiction tale of the future' do not tell us enough; we want to know more. But if we add: 'This piece comes' at the beginning, we have something that makes sense because we know what the words are about, and what happens.

Every sentence has a subject – what it is about – and a verb, which tells us what is going on. 'I've finished' is a complete sentence. 'I' is the subject and '(ha)ve finished' is the verb. In 'The master paused before replying' the subject is 'master' and 'paused' is the verb, telling us what he did.
– In the paragraph beginning 'For the first few days . . .' see if you can find the first two sentences.

Unit 14

Christmas

I would go out, my bright new boots squeaking, into the white world, on to the seaward hill, to call on Jim and Dan and Jack and to pad through the still streets, leaving huge deep footprints on the hidden pavements.

'I bet people will think there's been hippos.'

'What would you do if you saw a hippo coming down our street?'

'I'd go like this, bang! I'd throw him over the railings and roll him down the hill and then I'd tickle him under the ear and he'd wag his tail.'

'What would you do if you saw *two* hippos?'

Iron-flanked and bellowing he-hippos clanked and battered through the scudding snow toward us as we passed Mr Daniel's house.

'Let's post Mr Daniel a snowball through his letter-box.'

'Let's write things in the snow.'

'Let's write, "Mr Daniel looks like a spaniel" all over his lawn.'

Or we walked on the white shore.

'Can the fishes see it's snowing?'

The silent one-clouded heavens drifted on to the sea. Now we were snow-blind travellers lost on the north hills, and vast dewlapped dogs, with flasks round their necks, ambled and shambled up to us. We returned home through the poor streets where only a few children fumbled with bare red fingers in the wheel-rutted snow and cat-called after us, their voices fading away, as we trudged uphill, into the cries of the dock birds and the hooting of ships out in the whirling bay. And then, at tea the recovered uncles would be jolly; and the ice cake loomed in the centre of the table like a marble grave. Auntie Hannah laced her tea with rum, because it was only once a year.

Bring out the tall tales now that we told by the fire as the gaslight bubbled like a diver. Ghosts whooed like owls in the long nights when I dared not look over my shoulder; animals lurked in the cubbyhole under the stairs where the gas meter ticked. And I remember that we went singing carols once, when there wasn't the shaving of a moon to light the flying streets. At the end of a long road was a drive that led to a large house, and we stumbled up the darkness of the drive, each one of us afraid, each one holding a stone in his hand in case, and all of us too brave to say a word. The wind through the trees made noises as of old and unpleasant and maybe webfooted men wheezing in caves. We reached the black bulk of the house.

'What shall we give them? Hark the Herald?'

'No,' Jack said, 'Good King Wenceslas. I'll count three.'

One, two, three, and we began to sing, our voices high and seemingly distant in the snow-felted darkness round the house that was occupied by nobody we knew. We stood close together, near the dark door.

Good King Wenceslas looked out
On the feast of Stephen.

And then a small, dry voice, like the voice of someone who has not spoken for a long time, joined our singing: a small, dry, eggshell voice from the other side of the door: a small dry voice through the keyhole. And when we stopped running we were outside *our* house; the front room was lovely; balloons floated under the hot-water-bottle-gulping gas; everything was good again and shone over the town.

'Perhaps it was a ghost,' Jim said.

'Perhaps it was trolls,' Dan said, who was always reading.

'Let's go in and see if there's any jelly left,' Jack said. And we did that.

Always on Christmas night there was music. An uncle played the fiddle, a cousin sang 'Cherry Ripe', and another uncle sang 'Drake's Drum'. It was very warm in the little house. Auntie Hannah, who had got on to the parsnip wine, sang a song about Bleeding Hearts and Death, and then another in which she said her heart was like a Bird's Nest; and then everybody laughed again; and then I went to bed.

Looking through my bedroom window, out into the moonlight and the unending smoke-coloured snow, I could see the lights in the windows of all the other houses on the hill and hear the music rising from them up the long, steadily falling night. I turned the gas down, I got into bed. I said some words to the close and holy darkness, and then I slept.

A Child's Christmas in Wales: Dylan Thomas

A walk on Christmas morning

The slush of dirty feet.
A lonely seagull cries as it wheels,
Dark clouds linger overhead.

Here the party finished:
Empty glasses mourn on a coffee table
In the darkness of still-drawn curtains.
Spare rooms filled,
Five cars in drive;
Dining-room sleepers.
Here, a child awakes to find
That Santa Claus has been;
And there, a house left empty.
The partygoers are still asleep;
Drunken smiles adorn their faces.
Here, a wreath upon a door,
And there, a Christmas tree in window.
An early mother bastes the turkey.
In the lounge a family assembles
Exchanging presents, kisses and smiles.
In another, the deed being done,
Empty wrappings lie strewn around.

Small drops of rain ripple on the pond.
Even the dog senses the day.

Clive Wynn, aged 12

Comment

An adult remembers what Christmas was like when he was a boy, and a boy records his impressions on a morning walk. Dylan Thomas seems to recall just the right things – the way they imagined themselves lost in the snow and being rescued by St Bernard dogs, their fears, the bubbling and popping gaslight in the cosy home.

Clive is good at noticing the lifelessness after the Christmas Eve celebrations, before the world has fully woken up.

Christmas celebrates the birth of Christ, and that is important to Christians. The religious side of the festivities is often forgotten nowadays, but everyone enjoys a midwinter break and the chance for families to get together, while shops seize the opportunity to make some more money.

Activities

– How do you keep Christmas in your home? You may belong to a different religion and celebrate a festival at some other time, in which case write about that instead. Try to describe the atmosphere, mention some incidents, or give a diary of activities.
– Read St Luke, Chapter 2, verses 1-20, in the Bible. It is a rich and powerful story, whatever your beliefs. Write it as a newspaper article set in the present day.
– Design a Christmas card. Apart from drawing the picture, what words would you choose to have? Do you think the jingles found on the front or inside so many cards are helpful?
– Have you ever been carol-singing? Was it properly organized and for a charity, or did you just get together with some friends? If you had to choose four carols for a carol-singing expedition, which would you choose to learn?
– Read one of the most popular Christmas stories: Charles Dickens's *The Christmas Carol*. Do people like Scrooge still exist?

Nuts and bolts

Full-stops

These are the most important stop. If you learn how to use them and commas, you are not likely to have any complaints about your punctuation.

You already know about full-stops, because you use them every time you speak, at the end of each sentence. In writing we have to decide where sentences end, and this is usually easy. The difficulty for learners is remembering to use them. If in doubt, read your work aloud, or as nearly aloud as possible, and then you will feel where the stops should come.

Be ready to explain to a younger brother or sister or a beginner what full-stops are for. There are plenty of examples in our unit.
– Look through any written work you have done in the past week, and make sure that you have used full-stops where they are required.

Unit 15

Christmas in Space

A boy is on his first flight in space.

The rocket took off and they were flung headlong into dark space. They left Earth behind on which the date was December 24th, 2052, heading out into a place where there was no time at all, no month, no year, no hour. They slept away the rest of the first 'day'. Near midnight, by their Earth-time New York watches, the boy awoke and said, 'I want to go look out the porthole.'

There was only one port, a 'window' of immensely thick glass, of some size, up on the next deck.

'Yes, yes,' said the father.

The mother started. 'But–'

'I mean it,' said the father. 'I really mean it. Excuse me now. I'll be back.'

He left them for about twenty minutes. When he came back he was smiling. 'Almost time.'

'Can I hold your watch?' asked the boy, and the watch was handed over and he held it ticking in his fingers as the rest of the hour drifted by in fire and silence and unfelt motion.

'It's Christmas *now*! Christmas! Where's my present?'

'Here we go,' said the father, and he took his boy by the shoulder and led him from the room, down the hall, up a ramp-way, his wife following.

'I don't understand,' she kept saying.

'You will. Here we are,' said the father.

They had stopped at the closed door of a large cabin. The father tapped three times and then twice, in a code. The door opened and the light in the cabin went out and there was a whisper of voices.

'Not quite yet,' said the father. 'I'll take you up later.'

'I want to see where we are and where we're going.'

'I want you to wait, for a reason,' said the father. 'Son, in exactly one half-hour it will be Christmas.'

'Oh,' said the mother, dismayed that he had mentioned it. Somehow she had rather hoped the boy would forget.

The boy's face grew feverish and his lips trembled. 'I know, I know. Will I get a present? You promised–'

'Go on in, son,' said the father.

'It's dark.'

'I'll hold your hand. Come on, mama.'

They stepped into the room and the door shut, and the room was very dark indeed. And before them loomed a great glass eye, the porthole, a window four feet high and six feet wide, from which they could look out into space.

The boy gasped.

Behind him, the father and the mother gasped with him, and then in the dark room some people began to sing.

'Merry Christmas, son,' said the father.

And the voices in the room sang the old, the familiar carols, and the boy moved forward slowly until his face was pressed against the cool glass of the port. And he stood there for a long long time, just looking and looking out into space and the deep night at the burning and the burning of ten billion billion white and lovely candles.

The Day It Rained Forever: Ray Bradbury

Comment

The science fiction stories we find most satisfying are those in which the characters are human beings talking and behaving just like us, but in a strange setting. In this story, the boy and his parents await the coming of Christmas while on a space-flight to Mars.

Outside the Earth, time takes on a different aspect, and the travellers have to rely on their watches to know when it is Christmas. The mother seems anxious to conceal the fact that it is Christmas from her son, because it is going to be so unlike their normal celebrations; the boy's father, however, is intent upon making Christmas in space a memorable experience for him. Hearing Christmas carols and looking out of the porthole at the star-lit sky hold him spellbound.

Activities

– Make a list of what you would miss if you had to spend Christmas or another festival important to you in space. This may happen to you one day!
– How do you think the family's Christmas in space continued? Think of how limited in resources they would be; there isn't much room for luxuries in a space-ship. Write about the next quarter of an hour from when the boy has turned back from the porthole.
– Describe what you would consider to be your ideal Christmas or other important festival. Would it be at home, in a foreign land, in space? Would you want the traditional food? How would you pass the time?
– You meet a person from another planet who, fortunately, can speak English. He doesn't understand what Christmas is – neither in terms of its religious significance, nor in its social and commercial aspects. He is awkward, however, in having an in-built language processor which will allow him to accept only two hundred words of explanation from you. Write down what you would say to him.
– The early Christians imposed their Christmas celebrations on an old pagan midwinter festival. See if you can find out about this festival.

Nuts and bolts

Quotation marks

Quotation marks are sometimes known as Sixes and Nines (‘’) and sometimes as Sixty-sixes and Ninety-nines (“”). They are used to surround words actually spoken, when they are written down, or to put round words that have been quoted. The quotation marks surround everything, including stops: ‘I won't!’ and ‘We went in.’
– Find in our unit three examples of quotation marks placed outside stops; there are plenty.

Sixes and Nines (‘’) are nowadays used more often in printing than Sixty-sixes and Ninety-nines (“”) which are still used in writing.

Unit 16

Rex – the bull terrier

I ran across a dim photograph of him the other day, going through some old things. He's been dead twenty-five years. His name was Rex (my two brothers and I named him when we were in our early teens) and he was a bull terrier. 'An American bull terrier,' we used to say, proudly. He had one brindle eye that sometimes made him look like a clown and sometimes reminded you of a politician. The rest of him was white except for a brindle saddle that always seemed to be slipping off and a brindle stocking on a hind leg. Nevertheless, there was a nobility about him. He was big and muscular and beautifully made. He never lost his dignity even when trying to accomplish the extravagant tasks my brothers and myself used to set for him. One of these was the bringing of a ten-foot wooden rail into the yard through the back gate. We would throw it out into the alley and tell him to go get it. Rex was as powerful as a wrestler, and there were not many things that he couldn't manage somehow to get hold of with his great jaws and lift or drag to wherever he wanted to put them, or wherever we wanted them put. He would catch the rail at the balance and lift it clear of the ground and trot with great confidence toward the gate. Of course, since the gate was only four feet wide or so, he couldn't bring the rail in broadside. He found that out when he got a few terrific jolts, but he wouldn't give up. He finally figured out how to do it, by dragging the rail, holding on to one end, growling. He got a great, wagging satisfaction out of his work. We used to bet kids who had never seen Rex in action that he could catch a baseball thrown as high as they could throw it. He almost never let us down. Rex could hold a baseball with ease in his mouth, in one cheek, as if it were a chew of tobacco.

Swimming was his favourite recreation. The first time he ever saw a body of water (Alum Creek), he trotted nervously along the steep bank for a while, fell to barking wildly, and finally plunged in from a height of eight feet or more. I shall always remember that shining, virgin dive. Then he swam upstream and back just for the pleasure of it, like a man. It was fun to see him battle upstream against a stiff current, struggling and growling every foot of the way. He had as much fun in the water as any person I have known. You didn't have to throw a stick in the water to get him to go in. Of course, he would bring back a stick to you if you did throw one in. He would even have brought back a piano if you had thrown one in.

That reminds me of the night, way after midnight, when he went a-roving in the light of the moon and brought back a small chest of drawers that he found somewhere – how far from the house nobody ever knew; since it was Rex, it could easily have been half a mile. There were no drawers in the chest when he got it home, and it wasn't a good one – he hadn't taken it out of anybody's house; it was just an old cheap piece that somebody had abandoned on a trash heap. Still, it was something he wanted, probably because it presented a nice problem in transportation. It tested his mettle. We first knew about his achievement when deep in the night, we heard him trying to get the chest up on to the porch. It sounded as if two or three people were trying to tear the house down. We came downstairs and turned on the porch light. Rex was on the top step trying to pull the thing up, but it had caught somehow and he was just holding his own. I suppose he would have held his own until dawn if we hadn't helped him. The next day we carted the chest miles away and threw it out. If we had thrown it out in a nearby alley, he would have brought it home again, as a small token of his integrity in such matters. After all, he had been taught to carry heavy wooden objects about, and he was proud of his prowess.

The Middle-Aged Man on the Flying Trapeze:
James Thurber

Comment

Rex seems to have been quite a character. The family, of whom he was an important member, was clearly very fond and proud of him. His most remarkable characteristic was his physical strength, which, combined with his determination, enabled him to achieve astonishing feats. The word 'brindle' in the first paragraph means that Rex had brown patches on his eye, back and leg.

The writer affectionately endows Rex with qualities we normally associate with humans: Rex has 'a nobility about him', he never 'loses his dignity', he has 'integrity'.

Activities

– Do you know of a dog with a 'personality'? Can you think of a particular episode that shows the human quality? You could turn it into a story.
– There are many stories of dogs and their loyalty to humans; the dog is traditionally 'man's best friend'. Find out why, according to legend, the village of Beddgelert, in Wales, is so named; it's a moving story.
– Invent an episode for Rex. You could write as if you were one of the family or you could be the owner of another dog that doesn't see eye to eye with Rex!
– If you enjoy reading about dogs, try two novels by Jack London: *White Fang* and *The Call of the Wild*. Or his short story *To Build a Fire*.
– Some think that a dog should not be brought into a house, but should live in a kennel outside or in a basement. What are your views? Does it depend, perhaps, on the breed of dog – alsatians outside, poodles indoors?
– The police use dogs' abilities at following scents to track people and to discover drugs. Can you think of one or two other purposes for which we make use of dogs?

Nuts and bolts

Spelling
Notice what happens when '-ly' and '-ness' are added to words ending in 'l' and 'n':

    final + ly   = finally
    open   + ness = openness
    thin   + ness = thinness

Please note the following, however:

    full   + ly   = fully
    (three 'l's in a row would be a bit much!)

– Find in 'Rex' a word that goes just like 'final, finally' (fairly near the beginning).
  If you add '-ly' to a word ending in 'le', notice what happens:

    possible + ly = possibly

– Make up the rule for this and find another word that goes like it in 'Rex' (fairly near the end).
  One more ending, when a 'y' vanishes:

    busy   + ness = business
    lazy   + ness = laziness
    happy + ness = happiness

Unit 17

Haiku

Read these very short word-pictures carefully, letting your mind's eye imagine and enjoy the scene. You do not have to read them all at once, perhaps just four or five to begin with:

A sunny spring day,
People are doing nothing
In the small village.

No sky and no earth
At all. Only the snowflakes
Fall incessantly.

Through the town's centre
A little stream flows, bordered
By weeping willows.

Oh thin little frog
Don't lose the fight. Issa
Is right here to help.

On the temple bell
Something rests in quiet sleep.
Look, a butterfly!

A lovely spring day –
Out in the garden sparrows
Are bathing in sand.

On sweet plum blossoms
The sun rises suddenly.
Look, a mountain path!

The peasant hoes on.
The person who asked the way
Is now out of sight.

Into the old pond
A frog suddenly plunges.
The sound of water.

Snow having melted,
The whole village is brimful
Of happy children.

Up-swinging mattocks
Glittering in the sunshine!
Spring is in the fields.

The little rain frog
Rides on a banana tree
As it softly sways.

A brilliant full moon!
On the matting of my floor
Shadows of pines fall.

The faces of dolls.
In unavoidable ways
I must have grown old.

Comment

Though these poems are about a variety of subjects (snowflakes, sparrows, dolls, plum blossoms) they have one important fact in common: they are all translations from a traditional Japanese verse-form known as *haiku*. The basic pattern is three lines containing seventeen syllables, five syllables in the first line, seven in the second, and five in the third. There is no rhyme.

Usually there are two imagés or ideas which our imaginations link together; the poet offers us clues and we do the rest. Let us consider a *haiku* poem:

> **A**t every doorway,
> From the mud on the wooden clogs,
> Spring begins anew.

We picture the mud-covered clogs left at the door. The second idea refers to the arrival of spring. And the connection? Even the mud, not generally thought to be attractive, is a sign for rejoicing, since it means that the ground, frozen hard during the winter, has softened with the warmer weather; in short, the mud is a sign of the welcome spring.

Activities

— If you haven't been used to writing poems, try writing some in *haiku* form. It's a good way to start. Though our examples are mainly set out of doors, you don't have to stick to this.
— The American poet, Ezra Pound, was impressed with Oriental poetry and learnt a good deal from his reading. Here is a very short poem, *In a Station of the Metro*, that has the feel of *haiku* though it doesn't obey the syllable rules:

> **T**he apparition of these faces in the crowd;
> Petals on a wet, black bough.

(Metro = underground railway)

Jot down in your notebook what you think of it and what impression you think he wanted us to have.
— Find out about Matsuo Bashō, the greatest *haiku* writer of all time. He lived from 1644 to 1694.

— Ezra Pound, in a book called *ABC of Reading*, suggested some activities which could be useful as starting-points for poems or short descriptions:

> 'Let the pupil write the description of a tree without mentioning the name of the tree (larch, pine, etc.) so that the reader will not mistake it for the description of some other kind of tree.
>
> 'Try some object in the class-room.
>
> 'Describe the light and shadow on the schoolroom clock or some other object.'

He hasn't set easy tasks, but you might like to try.
— Sketch a scene suggested by one of the *haiku* we have printed.

Nuts and bolts

Spelling

In this section we are continuing to look at additions at the end of words, commonly known as suffixes. The important ones are: '-ing' and '-ed'. Often they are added without changing: melted, glittering, doing, bordered.

When '-ng' is added to a word ending in 'e' the 'e' is lost:

> ride   riding
> hope   hoping

— Find two examples of the vanishing 'e', one near the end of Comment, and one near the beginning of Activities.

Unit 18

A special occasion

A little boy and girl meet for the first time: the maid doesn't understand:

The door opened. A little brown-haired girl, in a party frock sticking out all round her legs like a lampshade, came in, stopped, and stared. Tom stared back at the girl.

Tom, having stared at the girl for a long time as one would study a curiosity, rare and valuable, put his feet together, made three jumps forward and said, 'Hullo.'

The little girl turned her head over one shoulder and slowly revolved on one heel. She then stooped suddenly and said, 'Hullo.'

Tom made another jump, turned round, pointed out of the window, and said in a loud voice something like 'twanky tweedle'. Both knew that neither the gesture nor the phrase was meant to convey a meaning. They simply expressed the fact that for Tom this was an important and exciting, a very special occasion.

The little girl took a step forward and said, 'I beg your pardon.'

They both gazed at each other for some minutes with sparkling eyes. Neither smiled, but it seemed that both were about to smile.

Tom then gave a shout, ran round the table, sat down on the floor and began to play with a clockwork engine on a circular track. The little girl climbed on a bike and pedalled round the floor.

Tom paid no attention. He was trying how fast the engine could go without falling off the track.

The little girl took a picture book, sat down under the table with her back to Tom, and slowly, carefully, examined each page. 'It's got a crooked wheel,' Tom said, 'that's what it is.' The little girl made no answer. She was staring at the book with round eyes and a small pursed mouth – the expression of a nervous child at the zoo when the lions are just going to roar. Slowly and carefully she turned the next page. As it opened, her eyes became larger, her mouth more tightly pursed, as if she expected some creature to jump out at her.

The door opened and the maid said, 'Tom, Tom, you naughty boy, is this the way you entertain you guests? Poor little Jenny, all by herself under the table.'

'She's not by herself,' Tom said.

'Oh, Tom, that really is naughty of you. Where are all your manners? Get up, and play like a good boy.'

'I am,' Tom said, in a surly tone, with a sidelong glance of anger.

'Now Tom, if you go on telling such stories, I shall know you are trying to be naughty. Get up now when I ask you.' She stooped, took Tom by the arm, and lifted him up. 'Come now, you must be polite.'

At this Tom instantly lost his temper and yelled, 'I won't – I won't.'

'Then I'll have to take poor Jenny downstairs again.'

'No – no – no.'

'Will you play with her, then?'

'No, I hate her.'

At this the little girl rose and said, in precise indignant tones, 'He *is* naughty, isn't he?'

Tom flew at her, and seized her by the hair; the little girl at once uttered a loud scream, kicked him on the leg, and bit his arm. She was carried screaming to the door.

Tom ran at the door and kicked it, rushed at the engine, picked it up and flung it against the wall. Then he howled at the top of his voice for five minutes. He intended to howl all day. He was suffering from a large and complicated grievance.

All at once the door opened and the little girl walked in. She had an air of immense self-satisfaction as if she had just done something very clever. She said in a tone demanding congratulation, 'I've come back.'

Tom gazed at her through his tears and gave a loud sob. Then he picked up the engine, sat down by the track. But the engine fell off at the first push. He gave another sob, looked at the wheels, and bent one of them straight.

The little girl lifted her frock behind in order not to crush it, sat down under the table, and drew the book on to her knee.

Tom tried the engine at high speed. His face was still set in the form of anger and bitterness, but he forgot to sob. He exclaimed with surprise and pleased excitement, 'It's the lines too – where I trod on 'em.'

The little girl did not reply. Slowly, carefully, she opened the book in the middle and gazed at an elephant. Her eyes became immense, her lips minute. But suddenly, and, as it were, accidentally, she gave an enormous sigh of relief, of very special happiness.

A Special Occasion: Joyce Cary

Comment

This is a story about young children written by an adult who knows very well how young children think and behave. The writer shows us how relationships have to begin naturally; two people don't get to know each other properly with a third person present – and relationships take time. Tom makes a display to show how pleased he is and Jenny comes to understand this. Then they both have to begin their own individual activity (Tom with his clockwork engine, Jenny with her book, having tried out the bike), each entering a private and happy world. The maid, interrupting, fails to see that they need to go through this stage. Tom's reaction shows his temper, a tantrum at having his 'special occasion' destroyed. Jenny's reaction is interesting: she agrees with the maid and responds to Tom's attack, but, by managing to return to the book and Tom, shows that she feels it's a 'special occasion' for her too.

Few people have maids nowadays, but when the writer of this extract was young, female servants were by no means uncommon.

Activities

– Did this story help you to remember a similar occasion when you were much younger? Think carefully; memories don't always come back quickly. Perhaps you can remember several incidents, once you start thinking.

– We all have occasions on which we feel we have been misunderstood. Is there one that upset you that you can write about? Very often, if we put something upsetting into words, it helps us cope with it.

– Imagine you know Tom well – perhaps he's your neighbour. He trusts you and tells you all about the episode from his point of view. What would you say to him?

– In our Comment we criticized the maid for failing to understand Tom's 'special occasion'. But we don't know what she had to put up with; Tom might well be most exasperating! Imagine her writing a letter to a friend that evening: 'That Tom, he drives me *mad*! Do you know, this afternoon . . .' Finish the letter.

Nuts and bolts

Adjectives

Adjectives give us information about things or people; they add to the meaning of a noun (or pronoun). Instead of saying 'a girl', the writer has added two adjectives: *little* and *brown-haired* to make 'a little, brown-haired girl'. Other examples in the story are *sparkling* eyes, a *circular* track, a *nervous* child. As you can see, the adjectives used here stand in front of the noun, but they don't have to; the writer could have written 'their eyes were *sparkling*', 'the track for the clockwork engine was *circular*' or 'she looked *nervous*'.

– Find four adjectives in the last paragraph of the story, two placed before their nouns, two after.

Unit 19

Lost on the hills

Four children are lost in a cold, wet mist on the Lake District fells.

'**W**ell, is *that* the top?'

Penny's voice carried a note of good-humoured despair, as if she had really given up hope.

Susan, a dim grey figure against the dim grey stones above, yelled back thinly against the wind:

'Can't see anything but mist! Half a tick, I'll run a bit and see what happens the other side!'

Then Tim, who for five minutes had not said a word, but had been a dogged shape plodding along the ridge, broke silence. For once he dropped his comfortable drawl. He shouted urgently:

'Don't be a fool, Susan! There may be a precipice the other side. Stop where you are, till we get up with you.'

'All right, Tim.'

And she stood there, unusually meek. And the wind roared and whined, driving the mist across like smoke from a bonfire, only more of it, and wet, and icy cold.

Tim looked round at Penny, struggling up the mountain behind.

'You all right?'

'You bet!'

Penny never complained – that was her pride. But she had already walked farther than she had bargained for, and the limp which showed so little in the ordinary way was getting more noticeable as she grew tired.

They went zigzagging up the grey slope in single file, first Tim with the rucksack, and then Penny, the moisture glinting on her black hair.

They never turned round to ask if *I* was all right. Now that I had handed over the rucksack to Tim, with all the food inside, I was free to fall over a precipice, sink into a bog, or just lie down and perish of exhaustion, as soon as I liked.

On the whole I preferred to plod on. 'Where are we?' I panted when I caught up with them.

Tim had the nerve to say: 'I haven't the faintest idea.'

'Well, I like that!'

'It's a good job you like it,' he said, dropping into his usual slow thoughtful way of talking, 'because even if you didn't, there isn't a fat lot we could do about it.'

Looking around me, I was inclined to agree. There was a monotonous quality about the scene. It consisted of fine grey grit, underfoot, sloping away in all directions at an alarming angle, until it vanished. Everything else was wet white fog, rushing across from left to right – and plenty more where that came from.

'Isn't this Black Banner, then?' asked my sister.

'I don't know, Sue.' Tim was struggling with the ordnance map, but it was hopeless in that wind. It flapped in his face like a frightened hen.

Penny blew on her knuckles. It was cold up there. 'If it *is* Black Banner,' she pointed out, 'it will very soon have a surplus of skulls and crossbones.'

Tim had given up the map as hopeless. He was now mumbling away over his compass.

'What use is the compass if we don't know where we're standing?' I said.

'It gives us our general direction, Bill,' said Tim in an injured tone. It was his compass – and his expedition. He was the local lad, as I kept reminding him.

'General direction!' I snorted. 'Fat lot of use in this country! Twenty miles due west should bring us to the seaside, and thirty miles due north should land us outside the main cinema in Carlisle! The fact that we should have broken our necks in the first mile —'

'I wish you boys would stop arguing,' said Penny. 'Come on, Sue. Let's get down somewhere out of this howling gale.' And she started to pick her way down the far side of the mountain.

We went after her, crouching and setting our feet carefully, like a bunch of old ladies with lumbago.

Once, for a few moments, the wind tore a gap in the curtain of mist. We got a sickening glimpse to our left – nothing whatever for about five hundred feet, and then a silvery thread of water spilling down over rocks at the bottom.

'When lost on the hills,' Tim quoted with a grim chuckle, 'find a stream and follow it down. No, thanks!'

I couldn't help feeling glad when the mist swirled over again, blotting out that sample of the landscape. The girls might have got nervous. To be quite honest, I didn't much like it myself.

Going down that mountain felt like walking on a house-roof, with a gale doing its best to blow you over the gutter into the street below.

'Snow here!' Penny called back.

And there it was, spreading over the side that faced north and missed the sun – a thin crisp layer of white, which must have been there for weeks. It was quite good fun, making the first footmarks across that snowfield.

When the snow began to thin out, the barren dust and chippings had given place to grass, wiry and poor, but somehow friendly.

The afternoon was wearing on. I reckoned that, without the mist, it would be dark in another hour. Goodness knows where we should find ourselves when we did get down. For the present, the important thing was to get anywhere off the tops.

Under Black Banner: Geoffrey Trease

Comment

There are two boys and two girls: Tim, the local lad; Penny, who knows little of the fells owing to an accident to her leg when she was small; Bill, the narrator of the story, and his sister, Susan, who have only been in the area for a year.

Notice how Bill and Tim react to each other. Bill seems rather sorry for himself. He feels that, now he has given the rucksack with the food in to Tim, no one is interested in his welfare: 'I was free to fall over a precipice, sink into a bog . . .' Bill becomes critical of Tim's handling of the expedition and, in particular, of Tim's lack of expertise in the use of map and compass.

Activities

– Describe the descent made by the four. Imagine the changes in mood and temper as the going becomes easier, the tracks wider and the surrounding more familiar.

– Penny's parents are anxious because the expedition ought to have returned an hour ago. Imagine the conversation as they wait.

– Write about Sue and Penny on the expedition. Do they seem more grown-up than the boys?

– Bill sits down that evening to write his diary. What would he have put? Draw an imaginary sketch map of the route.

– Have you ever been lost in the countryside, not necessarily on hills? If so, give a brief description of the area and try to remember how you felt. Did you find your own way back or were you found?

– Compile a list of rules for walking on hills or in open countryside. You will find that many books about climbing and mountain walking have such lists of 'do's' and 'don'ts'. Find out why it can be extremely dangerous to follow a stream. No wonder Tim says: 'find a stream and follow it down. No, thanks!'

– If one of the four had broken a leg on top of the mountain, what would have been the right course of action for the other three?

Nuts and bolts

Similes

On several occasions, to help us imagine more vividly, the author says that one situation is *like* another:

'the wind roared and whined, driving the mist across *like* smoke from a bonfire'
We are able to feel the choking thickness of the mist more easily.

'(the map) flapped in his face *like* a frightened hen'
The quick movement as the wind suddenly catches the map is well described.

'We went after her, crouching and setting our feet carefully, *like* a bunch of old ladies with lumbago'
You can imagine the four hunched over, finding it difficult to make progress.

When an author makes a comparison using *like*, we call it a *simile*.

– Look through the extract and find another example of a simile. Write it down and say, in a sentence, what the author is trying to achieve by using the simile. What sort of feeling is he trying to get across?

Unit 20

Something borrowed

It was a hot Saturday afternoon in July, and Bill Evans and Ronnie Evans and the gang had gone up Kilvey Hill to look for tadpoles. I was in my 'delicate' phase at the time, after having had a series of childhood illnesses one after the other. I had measles so quickly on top of chickenpox that the spots were fighting each other for space. Now I was getting over jaundice and was only allowed out near the house.

When Joyce Llewellyn came over to me I was reading a book of poetry by Keats which my grandfather had given me.

'Come on, Harry,' said Joyce, showering me with spit. 'We're playing weddings and you're the bridegroom.'

'I've been ill,' I said timorously, knowing the rigours of Joyce's games. 'Besides, my mother says I'm only to play near the front door.'

She tried another tactic.

'Mildred will be awfully upset,' she said. 'She's the bride.'

My head swam, and the book dropped from my lap. Mildred Reilly – the girl I worshipped from afar, the girl with the Shirley Temple dimples; whose 'Hello' could send me into a decline. . .

I submitted meekly to being led into position outside the tent, where the girls had set up an old packing case as an altar. Joyce stood in front of me with a tattered copy of *Pears Cyclopaedia* in her hands and behind me the other girls, acting as bridesmaids, sang *Here Comes the Bride* in three different keys. . .

'Do you take this woman to be your lawful wedded wife?' intoned Joyce from page 381 of *Pears Cyclopaedia*.

I nodded dumbly. 'Say "I do",' hissed the 'parson'.

'I do,' came croaking from my throat.

'Do you take this man to be your – er – lawful wedded husband?'

'I do,' whispered my beloved through the gaps in her teeth.

'Where's the ring?' spat Joyce.

'Here it is,' cried Ada Bayless, dropping her end of Mildred's frock and rushing forward with a gold ring. 'Be careful; it's my Mam's and she'll kill me if she finds I've pinched it.'

'Put it on her finger,' I was commanded.

Taking her hot, sticky little hand in mine I placed the ring on her finger where it dangled loosely. My heart was full and the rest of the ceremony was lost in a welter of happiness.

'I now pronounce you man and wife,' declared Joyce in a spray of triumphant spittle, shutting the book firmly. 'Kiss the bride,' she said.

Mildred lifted her cheek demurely, and with all the tenderness in my young world I kissed her.

'You're sweating,' said the girl who held my heart in her hands and rubbed her cheek vigorously where I had kissed it.

'Open the bottle of pop and get them broken biscuits,' Joyce was on the job again. 'Let's have the reception.'

'Let's have some then,' said my bride, leaving my side with an alacrity that hurt. All the other girls crowded round her giggling and chattering, leaving me bewildered and alone. They all crowded into the tent after the pop and biscuits. I stood uncertainly outside, feeling suddenly much older.

Then Mildred came out and offered me a drink from her cup. 'Use the other side,' she said. 'I've got lipstick on.'

Gratefully I accepted, not realising how thirsty I was, and before I had realised it I had drained the cup.

'You greedy thing,' she cried. 'You're only supposed to take a sip.' She slapped my face. 'I hate you. Old four eyes – old yellow face!' she chanted.

I couldn't see for tears. I stood biting my lip.

'I've been ill,' I blubbed through the opening in the tent. The other girls all giggled as I stuck my head inside.

'You wait,' I began; then, hearing footsteps behind me, I saw Billy Evans and Bob Jones holding jars full of tadpoles.

'Let's knock their tent down,' said Billy Evans, kicking at the broomstick supporting the back of it.

The girls shouted angrily inside as we pushed the tent over, and Joyce Llewellyn pummelled three of us as we pulled the blankets over their heads.

'You've spoiled the reception; you've ruined everything,' she cried hysterically, tears streaming down her face.

Mildred, my Mildred, ran sobbing to her house as I shouted, 'Serves you right, serves you right,' with a throat constricted with hatred and love all mixed up together.

Then my mother came out and called me in, and I went to bed early. I didn't have any supper, not because I was refused it, but because I didn't feel like it.

Something Borrowed: Harry Secombe

Comment

Harry Secombe says that this is his favourite story because it brings back memories of childhood in Swansea. 'The girl I "married" now has several children and has long since left the district. But it is still all there in my mind's eye. The agony of first love and the cruelty of children to one another, the very fabric of life itself.' Like some of the other writers from whom we have quoted in this book, Harry Secombe does not try to glorify the part he played.

Shirley Temple was a well-known child film star.

Activities

— Were you ever involved in a similar 'ceremony' when you were younger? What happened?
— Tell the story of an event that started with high hopes and ended in disappointment.
— Can you persuade an adult to tell you the most embarrassing experience in his or her childhood?
— Why do you think Harry Secombe entitled his story 'Something Borrowed'?
— If you had the opportunity to interview Harry Secombe for radio or television, what questions would you like to ask him?

Nuts and bolts

Adverbs

Adverbs add to the meaning of a verb, adjective or other adverb. They tell us how, why, when or where something happens. Examples from our unit are:

I had measles so *quickly*

I said *timorously*

Mildred will be *awfully* upset

Most adverbs end in '-ly', but a few like 'soon' and 'well' do not: *soon* finished, *well* done.
— Find the last adverb ending in '-ly' in the piece; it is fairly near the end.

Unit 21

A frightening experience

A boy and his tutor are being shown over a carpet mill by the overseer:

He was to dream, that night and for many nights to come, of what he saw during the next couple of hours.

It was not so much that the sights were frightening though some were that; but they were so strange, so totally unfamiliar compared with anything that he had ever seen before; the shapes and movements of the machines were so black, quick, ugly, or sudden; the noises were so atrociously loud, the heat was so blistering, the smells so sickly, acid or stifling. . . .

'Had enow, happen?' Scatcherd inquired drily, as they stood by the swiveller which spun and rocked so giddily that it made Lucas feel dizzy just to watch it. 'Reckon you've looked at as mooch as you can take for one shift?'

Lucas did feel so, but his pride was pricked by Scatcherd's tone.

'What was that thing you spoke of to Mr Smallside – the press? We haven't seen that yet, have we?'

'Oh, I think we've looked at quite enough for one evening –' Oakapple was beginning, but Scatcherd, again without appearing to hear the tutor, said, seeming to find this a most unexpected request, 'The press? You want to see the press? Eh – very well,' and he turned on his heel. 'Down this way then – pressing's the end of the manufacturing process. After that, the carpet's ready for sale. This here's the pressing room – careful down t'steps. They're slippery – t'glue gets all over.'

The pressing room was a huge place like the crypt of a church. Steps led down to it on all four sides.

'Where *is* the press?' Lucas began, and then, looking up, he saw that the whole ceiling was in fact a great metal slab which could be raised or lowered by hydraulic machinery.

A carpet was being unrolled and spread at feverish speed in the square central part of the room. The very instant it was laid out flat the men who had done so bounded up the steps, not a moment too soon, for the press came thudding down with a tremendous clap of dull sound.

'Toss a cobnut in there, you'll get it cracked free gratis,' Scatcherd said briefly.

Lucas could well believe him. If anyone slipped and fell under the press they would be done for. It rose up again much more slowly than it had come down, and the carpet was snatched away by a mechanical grab; then half a dozen overall-clad children with brooms, who had been waiting on the steps, darted out on to the floor and swept it with frantic speed and assiduity before the next piece of carpet was unrolled.

'Why can't the floor be swept by machinery?' Lucas asked.

'Children's cheaper,' Scatcherd answered laconically, with another of his sidelong glances. 'Machines has to be kept cleaned and oiled, but there's always a new supply o' kids.'

A question trembled in Lucas's mind but he couldn't bring himself to voice it.

'Isn't that job very dangerous?' he wanted to ask, but Scatcherd, as if hearing the unspoken words, went on, 'That bit's not *so* risky, but what does come up chancy is when there's a bit o' fluff or dirt discovered on the carpet when it's spread out – ah! Like there, see?'

A new carpet had been spread out, brown and gold; in the middle, clearly visible on a circle of gold, was a clot of black oily wool, seemingly left over from one of the previous processes.

'The chaps on the swiveller work too fast, you see; it often happens,' Scatcherd said. 'Now someone has to get it off, o'course, before it's ground in by t' press. The quickest one on the shift has to do it – the one they call the Snatcher. Watch now —'

A barefoot girl dashed out on to the carpet, snatched up a bit of wool with a pair of metal tongs, and leapt back to safety on the steps just before the great press thudded down again. She slipped a little on the steps, but recovered by throwing herself forward on to hands and knees, while two mates grabbed her arms.

Lucas took off his hat and rubbed his forehead with the back of his sleeve.

'O'course they gets paid a bit extra for snatching,' Scatcherd said. 'Ha'penny an hour danger money. Most of us has bin snatchers at one time or another when he was yoonger, but not for long – you can't keep on long at it, you gets nervous. You begin to dream at night, then your legs begins to shake and you can't run so fast.'

Lucas could imagine it. Just having seen the snatcher at work made him sick with fear. Mr Oakapple evidently shared this feeling.

'We have to go back,' he said abruptly. 'We have seen enough for this evening. Thank you.'

Midnight is a Place: Joan Aiken

Comment

Up to about a hundred and fifty years ago children were much employed in factories, mills and even mines. The hours were long, the work hard, and the conditions very harsh, so the health of the children suffered; some were crippled, some died. There were no laws to protect them; employers were often ruthless and brutal. Why did parents allow this cruelty to their children? The answer is that many of the children had no parents; and without factory work all would have faced starvation. Also wages were so low that children had to work to help the family finances.

We strongly recommend the book from which the extract is taken, and we wish we had more space to print about the visit to the factory; it is gripping to read, with its vivid descriptions of the dangers to life and limb for the child employees. The plot is exciting too: the girl and boy who are the chief characters survive some dreadful experiences before all ends well.

Activities

– What did Lucas write in his diary for the day of his visit? Remember that most diaries give very little space to each day.
– Imagine that the government of the time started an inquiry into child labour, and sent an inspector to interview young employees. What did one of them say about his working day of ten hours?
– Look back at the research you carried out in Unit 7, *The little sweep*, concerning the law and child labour.
– Write some notes on Lord Shaftesbury. What connection has he with Piccadilly Circus in London?
– Jot down a few lines about the kind of person Scatcherd was.
– Use a dictionary to find out the meaning of: atrociously, crypt, assiduity, laconically, abruptly. When you have read the definition, look back at the word in the passage to see how it fits in.

Nuts and bolts

Commas

Commas have several uses. One is to show the little pauses that we make in reading, especially in reading aloud. Another is to separate the items in a list of things.

Commas can be very important in documents like wills, where the placing of a comma can completely change the meaning, and lose or win a fortune for someone. Here is a correctly punctuated sentence from a local newspaper:

> At the tenants' ball the Duchess wore nothing to indicate that she was different from her guests.

The printer who added a comma after 'nothing' probably got into very hot water.
– Find all the commas in the first two paragraphs of our unit (from 'He was to dream . . .'). Then read the paragraphs aloud and see how the commas help.

Unit 22

The Listeners

'Is there anybody there?' said the Traveller,
    Knocking on the moonlit door;
And his horse in the silence champed the grasses
    Of the forest's ferny floor.
And a bird flew up out of the turret,
    Above the Traveller's head:
And he smote upon the door a second time;
    'Is there anybody there?' he said.
But no one descended to the Traveller;
    No head from the leaf-fringed sill
Leaned over and looked into his grey eyes,
    Where he stood perplexed and still.
But only a host of phantom listeners
    That dwelt in the lone house then
Stood listening in the quiet of the moonlight
    To that voice from the world of men:
Stood thronging the faint moonbeams on the dark stair
    That goes down to the empty hall,
Hearkening in an air stirred and shaken
    By the lonely Traveller's call.
And he felt in his heart their strangeness,
    Their stillness answering his cry,
While his horse moved, cropping the dark turf,
    'Neath the starred and leafy sky;
For he suddenly smote on the door, even
    Louder, and lifted his head: —
'Tell them I came, and no one answered,
    That I kept my word,' he said.
Never the least stir made the listeners,
    Though every word he spake
Fell echoing through the shadowiness of the still house
    From the one man left awake:
Ay, they heard his foot upon the stirrup,
    And the sound of iron on stone,
And how the silence surged softly backward,
    When the plunging hoofs were gone.

The Listeners: Walter de la Mare

Comment

There is a strong, eerie atmosphere in this poem. We imagine ourselves accompanying the Traveller on horseback up to the building with its door lit by the moon. We feel tense as he knocks on the door. And the champing of the horse, apparently unconcerned, emphasizes the surrounding silence and thereby adds to the tension. The sudden flight of the bird, disturbed by the knock, brings back a certain uneasiness which lasts until the Traveller gallops away after his third knock.

The poet builds up the atmosphere of silence and stillness by concentrating on the few sounds and movements that are heard and seen: the three knocks accompanied by the Traveller's voice, the horse eating, and the bird flying up. Then the burst of strong sound and vigorous movement at the end of the poem helps to leave us more content, for in a sense we feel that the man has escaped from the haunting silence, which seems living as it 'surges softly backwards'.

Activities

— Read the poem aloud as well as you can, listening to the sounds of the words. If you like the poem, write it out neatly in the anthology we recommended your compiling at the beginning of the book on page 9.

— Write a story indicating why the Traveller went on his visit. He says that he 'kept his word' which tells us that it was planned.

— The Traveller arrives home from his visit. As he stables and grooms his horse, what are his thoughts?

— You have been asked to produce a documentary film about Walter de la Mare. Find out about his life from reference books and read some of his poems. (Don't forget to copy out any you particularly like in your anthology.) You think an effective beginning of the film would be to show the Traveller knocking at the moonlit door. Write down some notes of description for the person responsible for finding a suitable location.

— Is there a house or some other building near you that has the reputation for being haunted? Find out as much as you can about it and make some notes. How much do you believe?

— Why are ghost stories so popular? Is it because we like to be frightened? Do you have a favourite story? Try writing a ghost story of your own. Your story might be about the house you considered in the last activity.

Nuts and bolts

Question marks

Question marks explain themselves: 'Where is the Post Office?' Note that there is no question mark in 'She asked where the Post Office was.' Only actual questions, written down as the speaker said them, need a question mark. How do we know in conversation that a person is asking a question?

Note how the question adds to the atmosphere of *The Listeners*. Try reading these:

> The Traveller asked if anybody was there,
>   Knocking on the moonlit door

and

> And he smote upon the door a second time;
>   He asked if anybody was there.

Then re-read the poem.

Unit 23

Astronomy

Man has studied the stars since the beginning of his time on earth. Even primitive man must have looked up into the heavens and been influenced by what he saw. In the ancient world the stars were supposed to govern men's lives. The horoscopes of early astrologers are echoed today in newspapers and magazines which tell their readers what experiences await them each week under their sign of the zodiac. The twelve constellations of the zodiac, which form the path of the sun as it appears to cross the sky, are very ancient.

Astrology led to astronomy, and it was often difficult to separate the two. This was particularly so in China where the first astronomers were very important people. They were called upon to make forecasts of such things as an eclipse of the sun, and if they made a mistake in their predictions they were condemned to death.

The ancient Greeks from the time of Thales of Miletus, a philosopher who lived in the 6th century BC, began to look at the universe scientifically. Euclid invented geometry; Eratosthenes measured the distance round the earth; and Hipparchus, the first real astronomer, made a close study of the heavens and established the position of over 850 stars.

After the Greeks, the Arabs took up astronomy. According to their religion all true believers must kneel and face in the direction of Mecca, the sacred city of Arabia, when they pray. One of the most important reasons why Arabic astronomy developed was to establish the geographical position of Mecca for the faithful, wherever they were in the world.

Modern astronomy began with Nicolaus Copernicus, a Polish astronomer who lived from 1473 to 1543. It was he who first demonstrated that the sun was at the centre of the solar system and not the earth, as had been previously believed. Tycho Brahe, a Danish scientist, who also lived in the 16th century, became so famous that the king of Denmark built him the finest observatory in the world on an island near Copenhagen, and called it the City of the Heavens.

But the most famous name in the history of early astronomy was that of Galileo, who died in 1642. Although he did not invent the telescope, Galileo was the first man to make proper use of it, and in 1609 he became the first person to see an object in the sky as it really was. When he published his astonishing discoveries about the universe he was put on trial by the pope, who said that his views were against the teaching of the church.

Another genius who devoted his life to science was Isaac Newton (1642–1727), who is remembered for the story of the falling apple in his garden, which is supposed to have set his mind thinking about the problems of gravitation. He probably did more than any other man to show that astronomy is a science based on scientific reasoning. He invented the principle of the reflecting telescope, which is now used in the world's largest optical telescopes.

Today, astronomers reach far beyond the range of ordinary telescopes which 'see' into the heavens. Radio telescopes, which receive radio waves from bodies in outer space, were first experimented with in the 1930s. The principle of the original bowl-type radio telescope has now been developed into new types which use many aerials and extend over large areas.

Hamlyn Younger Children's Encyclopaedia:
Kenneth Bailey

Comment

This is a general article on astronomy, attempting to give an outline of the progress made in astronomy from the earliest times to the present day. In all subjects, whether for school or for a hobby, it's a good idea to begin with an article like this to gain an overall impression, before looking more closely and in detail. In the Activities that follow, you will need to search for information in various encyclopaedias and reference books, as well as in books specifically on astronomy. The facts that you discover can be kept in your English folder or, if you find the topic of particular interest, you can begin a separate folder. Remember that astronomy can be a hobby that costs you nothing: all you need is access to a library and a night sky free of clouds!

Galileo's telescope

Activities

– Find out the names of the twelve constellations of the zodiac and the dates to which they refer. Discover as much as you can about your own sign. What type of character is your sign supposed to have? Do you think it applies to you?

– Four 'modern' astronomers are mentioned: Nicolaus Copernicus, Tycho Brahe, Galileo, Isaac Newton. Choose one of them and read up about him.

– What is the difference between an ordinary telescope and the reflecting telescope invented by Isaac Newton? How does a modern radio telescope work? Draw diagrams to help your explanations.

– There are many books available illustrating the sky at night. Find a suitable illustration and then, on a clear night, see how many constellations you can identify. The constellations are named after characters in mythology. One such character is Pegasus, the winged horse, that you can read about in Unit 50. What shape does his constellation make?

– Try to explain to a friend how you can find the Pole Star and say why it is important as a star.

– In Shakespeare's play *Romeo and Juliet* the following lines are spoken:

ROMEO *Lady, by yonder blessed moon I swear That tips with silver all these fruit-tree tops —*

JULIET *O, swear not by the moon, the inconstant moon . . .*

(Act 2 Scene 2)

Why does Juliet say that the moon is 'inconstant'? You will need to read about the moon and its movements. Juliet's next line gives a clue!

– How is there a connection between the moon and the sea?

– Why is the study of the stars called 'astronomy'? Look in a dictionary that has derivations, that is, in a dictionary that tells you how words came into English. What other words are derived from the same source?

Goonhilly Satellite earth station

Nuts and bolts

Paragraphs

Paragraphs usually start with a sentence that tells us what is coming. This is often called the 'topic' sentence because it mentions the subject or 'topic' of the paragraph. Occasionally this sentence comes at the end of the paragraph, and sums up what has gone before.

– Look carefully at the first four paragraphs of our unit. In each case, does the first sentence actually tell us what the paragraph is about? Decide what each paragraph is about and see if you agree that paragraphs usually start with a 'topic' sentence.

Unit 24

Robert goes exploring

It is a Saturday afternoon in winter. Robert is indoors with his mother:

The fire burnt red in the house, and the coldness from outside fell into the room at the window.

'I'll be glad when it's dark, and we can draw the curtains,' said Mum.

'Hmn,' said Robert. He was roasting himself side by side by the fire, not comfortable, and not wanting to be. Michael had gone out after dinner, pulling on his new gloves. Robert had stayed in, because Mum had called him back. She had really meant to call Michael back and say something about the gloves, but she had said the wrong name.

'Now you don't even know which is which,' said Robert. 'I suppose it's my turn next.'

'It will be if you don't look out,' said Mum. But Michael had gone, and wasn't there to be told anything.

'What are you miserable about?' said Mum.

'Michael's always going out,' said Robert.

'He's getting a big boy now,' said Mum. 'He wants to be with his friends.'

'So do I,' said Robert.

'Go on with you,' said Mum. 'He has to go his own way now, you know.'

Robert thought that must have one meaning: Michael was being let go of; he had been brought up, and his time was coming to leave home.

'Now get up from there,' said Mum. 'Go and get me a pot of paste for your father's tea. Salmon it is he likes.'

'All right,' said Robert, getting up half-cooked, or stiff one side and melting the other. He put on his coat, and then realised that if he went out for paste he could go to other places too. He went out into the cold. It sank through his cheeks and hurt his teeth and his nose suddenly ran.

He bought the paste first, because that was his errand. Instead of going home he went on through the middle of the town, and out towards the mill.

No one watched him go. No one noticed him. And no passer-by halted to look at him and say 'You are on your way to do something wrong,' and that was surprising, because he felt his intention walking along beside him as large as himself.

The road by the mill was empty. Robert looked at the railing. He felt it. It was cold. It was glazed with frost. He put a foot half-way up, another foot on the top rail, and his elbow on the wall top. He wriggled. He was on the wall. The pot of paste rattled on the brickwork. He took it from his pocket and looked at it. It had not chipped. He stood on the wall. He could see the wide gutter of the chapel, and beyond it the houses of the town, quite far away, as if there were a big field between him and them.

He climbed on to the roof, dusted his knees, which were grimy with the town frost, and stood up. He walked a little way along the gutter which joined the wall of the mill.

Someone walked in the road, and went past the entry. Robert looked round the corner of the mill. He saw feet go by. No one saw him. He thought they might have felt he was there by other means than seeing. He felt too real.

He found what he had begun to expect. A door. A door into the mill. He pushed it. It swung open. Beyond it was darkness. He stepped through, and left the daylight. He pushed the door shut behind him, but kept his hand on it in case he had to go out again at once. He stood with his back to it, looking and listening.

He began to see light. It came from a window that was out of sight. He heard noises. There were voices. And there was hammering.

He let go of the door, and moved to the edge of the floor. Down below was the bottom of the mill. It was from below that the sounds came. There was a ladder. He felt it to see that it was firm, and went down it.

Pig in the Middle: William Mayne

Comment

Robert experiences the frustration that many children with older brothers and sisters feel: the world outside, the life of increasing independence, is far more exciting than life at home. Michael enjoys being out with friends, while poor Robert is left miserable and discontented indoors. Being sent out to buy salmon paste for his father's tea gives him just the opportunity he wants to go exploring. Notice how, when he first goes outside, the cold hurts him; but he soon warms up with the excitement of the adventure.

We have deliberately left the episode at the moment when Robert must have felt two strong

emotions: fear, because he is not where his mother thinks he is and he is in a somewhat dangerous position, and intrigue, because he would clearly love to know whose voices he could hear and what the people were hammering.

Activities

– Continue Robert's story. Does he find out to whom the voices belong? Does the pot of salmon paste arrive home in time for his father's tea? The possibilities for continuing are many, of course. Try to finish the story plausibly. (If you haven't come across 'plausibly' before, look it up in a dictionary.)

– To find out what really happened, you will have to read William Mayne's novel. You should be able to find a copy easily.

– Have you ever been sent on an errand and then decided to do something different? If so, write down as vividly as you can how you felt when you made the decision. You might like to turn this into a short story, inventing the name of a character rather than writing as if it were you.

– The road and the mill seemed deserted. Have you ever looked at an old building – an old house, perhaps, or a disused factory – and wondered what it would have been like years before, when inhabited? There may be somewhere near your home. If so, describe it in detail as it is now, then write a contrasting piece imagining what it might have been like in its heyday.

– Write a spine-chilling story, set in an old building, that takes three to five minutes to read aloud. When you are satisfied with it and have tried reading it aloud to see how it flows, find some suitable sound effects to accompany it, and then record the story and effects on a cassette. It might be easiest to ask a friend to operate the sound effects while you read the story.

Nuts and bolts

Spelling

Syllables are the small units of sound which make up words. 'Fire', 'burnt' and 'red' all have one syllable each. 'Robert', 'indoors' and 'mother' have two: 'comfortable' and 'suddenly' have three.

It is a great help with spelling long words to say them aloud, dividing them up and pronouncing every syllable.

– Say these aloud, syllable by syllable: independence, discontented, opportunity, deliberately, accompany.

Unit 25

Billy

To Billy school was only an opportunity for fighting; and when the other boys set on him, he puts them all to flight:

I stood alone on the cobbles and a wave of passionate sorrow engulfed me. Indignation and affront, shame and frustration took command of my muscles and my lungs. My voice rose in a sustained howl, for all the world as though I had been the loser. . .

I cut my crying to a whimper and settled to the business of getting it home. Past the Aylesbury Arms, across the London Road, through Oxford Street by the Wesleyan Chapel, turn left for the last climb in the Green – and there my feelings inflated like a balloon, so that I did the last twenty yards as tragically as I could have wished, swimming through an ocean of sorrow, all quite genuine – swung on the front-door knob, stumbled in, staggered to my mother . . .

'Why, Billy! Whatever's the matter?'
. . . balloon burst, floods, tempests, hurricanes, rage and anguish – a monstrous yell . . .

'THEY DON'T LIKE ME!'

My mother administered consolation and the hesitant suggestion that perhaps some of the transaction had been my own fault. But I was beyond the reach of such footling ideas. She comforted, my father and Lily hovered, until at last I was quiet enough to eat. My mother put on her enormous hat and went out with an expression of grim purpose. When she came back, she said she thought everything would be all right. I continued to eat and sniff and hiccup. I brooded righteously on what was going to happen to my schoolfellows now that my mother had taken a hand. They were, I thought, probably being sent to bed without anything to eat, and it would serve them right and teach them to like me and not be cruel. After lunch I enjoyed myself darkly inventing possible punishments for them – lovely punishments.

Miss called later and had a long talk with my mother in the drawing-room. As she left I stuck my head round the dining-room door again and saw them.

'Bring him along a quarter of an hour late,' said Miss. 'That's all I shall need.'

Next day at school everyone was seated and you could have stuck a fork into the air of noiseless excitement. Wherever I looked there were faces that smiled shyly at me. I inspected them for signs of damage but no one seemed to have suffered any crippling torment. I reached for a rubber, and a girl in pink and plaits leaned over.

'Borrow mine.'

A boy offered me a handkerchief. Another passed me a note with 'wil you jine me ggang' written on it. I was in. We began to say our tables and I had only to pause for breath before giving an answer to six sevens for a gale of whispers to suggest sums varying from thirty-nine to forty-five. Dear Miss had done her work well, and today I should enjoy hearing her fifteen minutes' sermon on brotherly love. Indeed, school seemed likely to come to a full stop from sheer excess of charity; so Miss, smiling remotely, said we would have an extra long break. My heart leapt, because I thought that now we could get on with some really fierce, friendly fighting, with even a bloody nose. But Miss produced a train set. When the other boys got down to fixing rails, the girls, inexpressibly moved by the sermon, seized me in posse. I never stood a chance against those excited arms, those tough, silken chests, those bird-whistling mouths, that mass of satin and serge and wool and pigtails and ribbons. Before I knew where I was, I found myself, my eyes popping out of my head, playing Postman's Knock.

The first girl to go outside set the pattern.

'A parcel for Billy Golding!'

In and out I went like a weaver's shuttle, pecked, pushed, hugged, mouthed and mauled, in and out from fair to dark to red, from Eunice who had had fever and a crop, to big Martha who could sit on her hair.

I kissed the lot.

This was, I suppose, my first lesson; and I cannot think it was successful. For I did not know about the sermon then. I merely felt that the girls and boys who tried to do democratic justice on me had been shown to be wrong. I was, and now they knew it, a thoroughly likeable character. I was unique and precious after all, and I still wondered what punishments their parents had found for them which had forced them to realize the truth.

I still refused to do my lessons, confronting Miss with an impenetrable placidity. I still enjoyed fighting if I was given the chance. I still had no suspicion that Billy was anything but perfect. At the end of term, when I went down to Cornwall, I sat in a crowded carriage with my prize book open on my knees for six hours, so that passengers could read the inscription. I am reading it now:

Billy Golding 1919 Prize for General Improvement

Billy the Kid: William Golding

Comment

The boy described here was spoiled and flattered by his mother, who said in front of him that his eyes were cornflower blue and his hair was like a field of ripe corn. He had known no one outside the family, loved collecting words as others might collect stamps and had no use for figures.

The description is autobiographical; the author is writing about himself. It is an honest account; it leaves the impression that so far from trying to give a favourable picture of himself, William Golding has gone to the other extreme and shown us a selfish and unpleasant little tough. But he is not really tough, for he 'blabs' and 'blubs' more than most.

Activities

– 'Miss' owns the school, and she keeps a diary about it. What did she put in for the two days described here?

– What did Mrs Golding say to Miss at the Golding's house? Write it as a conversation.

– Very little indeed is said about Billy's father, but there is enough to give an indication. What sort of person was he?

– Imagine one of the girls sitting down after tea chatting about her day to an elder sister about Billy. What might she have said?

– Early in the piece Billy settles to the business of 'getting it home'. What is 'it' and what does this tell us about Billy?

– Look up in a dictionary: affront, frustration, sustained, inflated, placidity. Having done that, look at each word in turn and see how it is used in the extract.

– If you have any views on prizes, put the pros and cons (arguments for and against) in note form and set out as a table (in much the same way you set out the third activity of *The riddle of Loch Ness*, Unit 11).

Nuts and bolts

Spelling

The method of building up and breaking down that we suggested in Unit 24 is a very good one, and we want to underline it. Long words are not at all alarming when we see how they are built up. For instance 'opportunity' easily breaks down into 'op/port/unity'.

– In the same way try breaking down these words into bits that you can say separately:

intercontinental semi-articulated vehicles

and from the unit:

indignation, frustration, inexpressibly, democratic, impenetrable.

Unit 26

English words

Our language is made up of bits from all over the place; that is why its spelling may seem difficult.

In the years before Christ the inhabitants of England were called Celts, or Ancient Britons. Only a very few of their words have survived, such as *glen* and *bard* – the word for their poets, who led them in times of trouble. Then came the Romans, who made England into a colony and farmed on a large scale. They departed after four hundred years, leaving behind these farms, some fortified camps and some excellent paved roads; we still have the names of some, like the Fosse Way and Ermine Street. But otherwise only three or four words of their tongue have survived to this day: *port, street* and the word for camp – *castra* – which lives on in the names of many places like Lancaster, Chester and Gloucester. Many towns show by their names that they were built near Roman roads or 'streets': Chester-le-Street, Stratford, Street (in Somerset), Stratton, Stretton, etc. They measured distances on these roads in *milia* (thousands – of paces), from which we get our *mile*.

Three more invasions brought in thousands of the words which give our language so much of its strength. As the Roman legions marched home, the Saxons and Angles arrived, giving us our name, *English*. At first they came as raiders and plunderers, but they settled down and farmed, burning off the forest in some places. This gives us names with *ash* in them: Ashford, Ashwell, Ashbocking. These Anglo-Saxons are our ancestors, and their language developed into the one we use now. The speech of the original Britons survived only in Scotland (Gaelic) and Wales (Welsh). The Anglo-Saxon tongue probably sounded rather like modern German. They gave us many of the words for our world: *night, wind, star* and *dew*; and for the way we live, and our food and shelter. So *man, wife* and *child eat, drink* and *sleep* in *houses*; they *love* and *hate*; they used to *till* their *land* and *harvest* their *crops*. Anglo-Saxon words are short and good at conveying vigorous action: *break, gasp, smart, slay, hurt, swear, run, fight*. Hundreds of names for plants and animals, the weather and farm-work are Anglo-Saxon; so

are many names; in surnames like Harding, Downing, Manning, Spurling and Browning the *ing* part means 'son of'. Finally they gave us names for parts of the body, and our handy habit of tacking *-er* on to the end of a word to indicate the doer of an action: *baker, thatcher, tiler, writer*.

Here is a sample of Anglo-Saxon: the beginning of the Lord's Prayer, in modern English 'Our Father who art in Heaven, hallowed be thy name':

> Faeder ure,
> thu the eart in heofonum,
> si thin nama gehalgod . . .

Being very much men of action, our ancestors had not much time for writing, and nearly every bit of their writing we have was set down by monks. They did have literature, though, most of it poetry to make it easy to remember and recite in the dark winter evenings. It includes riddles, charms, religious verse, accounts of battles, and a long story in verse about Beowulf and his fights against monsters and dragons. All this literature is contained in four books, written by hand; one of them, the Exeter Book, was given to Exeter Cathedral library nearly a thousand years ago. It is still there, and you can see it, if ever you visit Exeter.

The next invasion was spread over the two hundred years before the Normans came. The invaders were from Scandinavia; known as Danes at the time, they have also been called Vikings and Norsemen. They killed and plundered and destroyed, almost for the sake of destroying, but eventually they settled down and merged with the English. They gave us a number of useful words, such as *husband, knife, skin, take, want, law* and *wrong*. They provided us with pronouns: *they, them, their, she*; and they invented the good idea of adding 's' to words, for two purposes: first to express the plural: *games, roads*, etc., and secondly to show possession: *dog's dinner, cat's basket*, etc.

The third invasion, and the last to succeed, was the Norman Conquest of 1066. Then for a long time England was a country of two languages. The business of government and the law courts was carried on in Norman French, the language of the conquerors, while the ordinary people, the conquered, went on talking English. The English serfs spent their time looking after *oxen, sheep, calves* and *swine*, but when the Norman lords had their dinner at night they fed on these things by different names: *beef, mutton, veal, pork* and *bacon*. Life in the great castles was carried on in Norman words like *master, servant, butler, dinner*, terms used by the *dukes, viscounts, barons* and *countesses*. Killing and wounding were also described in Norman words: *arms, assault, battle, siege* and *war*.

Here is a riddle from the Exeter Book, put into modern English: one solution has eight letters, describes a migrant bird, and begins and ends with 's':

The wind carries little creatures
Over the rocky hills. They are
Black and swarthy in their dark coats,
Singing loudly, generous with their songs,
Travelling about in numbers together,
They live in wooded cliffs, yet sometimes
They visit the towns and houses of men.
They name themselves.

Comment

Some people get very interested in words, where they come from, and their history. They enjoy the feeling that when they use words like 'street' and 'port', they are echoing speakers who lived two thousand years ago. If you hear someone talking about his *salary*, he is using the Roman word for soldiers' pay; it means 'money for salt', a thing not easy to come by in those days. And if you walk along a Roman road in the country, it is easy to imagine a legion marching along, led by a man with a big trumpet. In a later book we shall be looking at a few of the thousands of words that have been imported since the Normans settled down and our English began to be spoken.

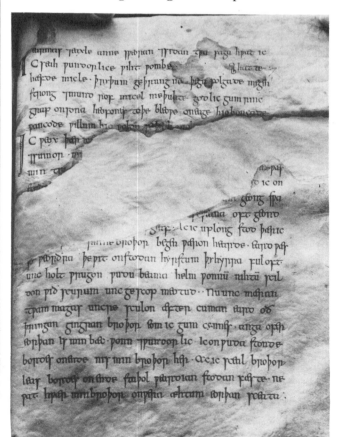

Activities

—Make a summary of 'English words'. Read it again; then write your summary of thirty or forty words without looking at the original. Or try another method: jot down half a dozen notes as you read, and then write them up.
—Look at a large-scale map of part of England, and find as many Roman roads as you can. What do you notice about them? Then look for places on these roads, with *strat*, or *stret*, or *cester* in them.
—Ask the Librarian for a dictionary of surnames, and look up your own surname and those of your friends.
—If you can get hold of a dictionary that gives the origins of words, try to find out the derivation of: *lady, gospel, daisy, dandelion* and *window*.
—Here are two groups of words, one English, the other Norman: (1) castle, arches, columns, tower; (2) house, beams, hearth, stool. Which is which? By now you will have given the right answer, but why did you choose?

Nuts and bolts

Plural means 'more than one'. The usual method of telling us that there are more than one of a thing is to add 's': bits, inhabitants, years, Celts, Britons. Remember words like 'businesses' and 'matches' in which the sound tells us that an 'e' is needed.

Words ending in 'f' and 'fe' usually go like this:

life	lives
shelf	shelves
half	halves

Some do not change at all:

chief	chiefs
relief	reliefs
roof	roofs

With some you can do as you like:

handkerchief   handkerchiefs or handkerchieves
hoof   hoofs or hooves

With all these words it is a matter of the right habit, and most people get the right habit without thinking about it.
—Say the plurals of these words, and you will get them right automatically: cliff, knife, safe.

A damaged page in the Exeter Book

Unit 27

Fact and fiction

Mr Farthing's lesson on fact and fiction is interrupted by the return of Billy Casper from a painful interview with the headmaster. The class has given sensible answers to the teacher's request for facts about Anderson; and then Mr Farthing turns to Anderson himself:

'All these are facts about Anderson, but they're not particularly interesting facts. Perhaps Anderson can tell us something about himself that *is* interesting. A really interesting fact.'

There was a massive 'Woooo!' from the rest of the class. Mr Farthing grinned and rode it; then he raised his hands to control it.

'Quietly now. Quietly.'

The class quietened, still grinning. Anderson stared at his desk, blushing.

'Don't know owt, Sir.'

'Anything at all, Anderson, anything that's happened to you, or that you've seen which sticks in your mind.'

'I can't think of owt, Sir.'

'What about when you were little? Everybody remembers something about when they were little? It doesn't have to be fantastic, just something that you've remembered.'

Anderson began to smile and looked up.

'There's summat. It's nowt, though.'

'It must be if you remember it.'

'It's daft really.'

'Well tell us then, and let's all have a laugh.'

'Well it was once when I was a kid. I was at Junior school, or somewhere like that, and went down to Fowlers Pond, me and this other kid, Reggie Clay they called him, he didn't come to this school; he flitted and went away somewhere. Anyway it was Spring, tadpole time, and it's swarming with tadpoles down there in Spring. Edges o't pond are all black with 'em, and me and this other kid started to catch 'em. It was easy, all you did was to put your hands together and scoop . . . we were on about bringing some home, but we'd no jam jars. So this kid, Reggie, says, "Take thi wellingtons off and put some in there, they'll be all right till thee gets home." I says to this kid,

"Let's have a competition, thee have one welli and I'll have t' other and we'll see who can get most in!"

'You ought to have seen 'em, all black and shiny, right up to t' top. When we finished we kept dipping our fingers into 'em and whipping 'em up at each other, all shouting and excited like. Then this kid says to me, "I bet tha daren't put one in." And I says, "I bet tha daren't." So we said we'd put one on each. We wouldn't though, though we kept reckoning to, then running away, so we tossed up and him who had lost had to do it first. And I lost, oh, and you'd to take your socks off an' all. So I took my socks off, and I kept looking at this welli full of taddies, and this kid kept saying, "Go on then, tha frightened, tha frightened." I was an' all. Anyway I shut my eyes and started to put my foot in. Oooo. It was just like putting your foot into live jelly. They were frozen, and when my foot went down, they all came over t' top of my wellington, and when I'd got my foot to t' bottom, I could feel 'em all squashing between my toes.'

'Anyway I'd done it, and I says to this kid, "Thee put thine on now." But he wouldn't, he was dead scared, so I put it on instead. I'd got used to it then, it was all right after a bit; it sent your legs all excited and tingling like. When I'd got 'em both on I started to walk up to this kid, waving my arms and making spook noises; and as I walked they all came squelching over t' tops again and ran down t' sides. You ought to have seen him. He just screamed out and ran home roaring.'

'It was a funny feeling though when he'd gone; all quiet, with nobody there, and up to t' knees in tadpoles.'

Silence. The class up to their knees in tadpoles. Mr Farthing allowed them a pause for assimilation. Then, before their involvement could disintegrate into local gossip, he used it to try to inspire and emulate.

'Very good, Anderson. Thank you. Now has anyone else anything interesting to tell us?'

No hands went up.

'No? What about you, Casper?'

Billy was bending over, inspecting his hands under cover of the desk. Pink weals were stamped across his fingertips. When he opened his fingers the weals broke into segments; each segment resembling a bump of nettle-rash. He blew on them, and cooled them with his tongue.

'Casper!'

Billy sat up and put his hands away.

Kestrel for a Knave: Barry Hines

Comment

Kes is the story (made into an excellent film) of a boy's friendship with a kestrel; and it wasn't easy to be friends with a wild bird of prey. With so many ponds being filled up by farmers and builders it would not be so easy now to find such quantities of tadpoles, and perhaps not so many boys nowadays would go in for a dare of this kind. But we can agree with Mr Farthing that Anderson's tale was worth telling and worth listening to; that is why he encouraged the rest of the class to have a go.

Activities

– What would be your answer if anyone asked you to tell them something interesting that had happened to you?
– What would happen today if anyone discovered a pond well supplied with tadpoles?
– Have you read or seen on television anything so realistic that you felt an impression like that of Billy's class – 'up to their knees in tadpoles'? If so, describe it.
– What was it that Mr Farthing liked so much about Anderson's talk?

– Where in the passage does it say something like. 'He gave them time to let it sink in'?
– Try one of these books about friendships with animals: Grey Owl: *Sajo and her Beaver People*; M.K. Rawlings: *The Yearling* (a fawn); R. Guillot: *Kpo the Leopard*; P. Fitzgerald: *Jock of the Bushveld* (a terrier).

Nuts and bolts

Apostrophes

Apostrophes are needed for two purposes. The first is to show that a letter or letters have been dropped out, as in:

it's	= it is
I've	= I have
you've	= you have
aren't you	= are not you
might've	= might have

Make quite sure of the first and last; and say aloud the full form of each of: we'll, you'd better, I should've, you can't, we'd go . . .
– Find three examples of apostrophes used for missing letter(s) in the unit; Anderson's story will supply plenty.

The other use of apostrophes we shall discuss in Unit 45.

Unit 28

Once there was a king...

Once there was a king who promised he would never chop anyone's head off. He ruled over a very noisy court. Everyone made a noise. They laughed and shouted and sang. They coughed. They hiccupped. They banged and thumped. They booed. They whistled and cheered.

Now, the king didn't like the noise, and he wanted to stop it. So, he thought a bit, and he walked a bit. He thought a bit more – and then he had a plan.

'The next one of you to make a noise will die!' he said.

Everyone went quiet, even though they all knew this king would never chop anyone's head off.

Everyone was quiet – except in one corner, and there was the boy who scrubbed the pots and pans in the kitchen. He was new to the court, and he made a noise and laughed. He liked noise.

The king looked at him. Everyone looked at him. He laughed again.

'Boy! Leave the hall!' the king said.

So the boy picked himself up and went off to the kitchens.

'Guards!' the king shouted. 'Lock the doors!'

The guards locked the doors. The king sat and waited. The court sat and waited. Outside, the boy banged his saucepan and sang.

Up and down,
Up and down,
Tim Tom Tackler
Goes up and down.

A whole hour went by. Not a sound came from inside the hall. Dinner time came, and still everyone was quiet. But outside they could hear the boy's song.

Up and down,
Up and down,
Tim Tom Tackler
Goes up and down.

Everyone was quiet, and now they could hear the boy eating. They could hear the sound of a ladle hitting the big soup cauldron. Like a great bell it was. They heard the soup go slosh into his

bowl. They heard him sipping at his spoon. And the ones nearest the door heard the soup gurgling in his belly.

Still they sat.

They heard the sound of sausages sizzling in the pan. They smelt the sausages. They saw the smoke coming under the door, and the ones nearest the door even heard him sprinkling salt and pepper on them.

Still they sat.

They heard the sound of a knife cutting cake, the crack of the icing, and the swish through cream. They heard him smacking his lips and licking his fingers, and the ones nearest the door even heard him picking up the crumbs.

> Eat a bit,
> Tim Tom Tackler.
> Eat a bit
> Tackler Tom.

The people in the court were going mad with hunger. What was the king up to?

Just when it seemed as if everyone was going to burst, the king spoke to the guards.

'Guards, open the doors!'

Then he turned to the court and spoke again.

'You may go,' he said.

Like a great fierce dragon, they rushed out of the hall, down the steps, round the corner, and into the kitchen where the boy was finishing his dinner. And, like one fierce dragon, they leapt on the boy and pulled him apart.

'Dinner, dinner, dinner,' some shouted.

'Drink, drink, drink,' others shouted.

Upstairs the king waited.

Soon his court came rushing back.

'We got him,' some shouted. 'We did for him!'

And the king who never ever chopped people's heads off spoke.

'The next person to make a noise will die.'

This time, they did as they were told, and they all went very quiet.

Once There Was A King Who Promised Never to Cut Anyone's Head Off: Michael Rosen

Comment

On the surface this story resembles a rather nasty 'once upon a time' fairy story that children enjoy hearing from quite an early age. It is based, however, on an idea rather than on an experience. There are several interesting, if horrible, aspects to the story which we would like you to consider.

First, let's think about the king. He has a poor understanding of how to rule, making no attempt to express his dissatisfaction at the noises of his subjects before issuing his vicious, and quite unreasonable, threat. It seems as if he knew in advance what would happen to the poor boy who scrubbed the pots and pans. After all, he thought, devised his plan, and then announced what would happen to the next person who made a noise.

The behaviour of the people in the court shocks us. They sound an unruly mob at the beginning; shouting, thumping, and booing. And they become savage.

Notice how the author describes so vividly the boy eating his food. This is calculated to make us appreciate how ravenously hungry the people in the court had become.

Activities

—Write the news item about this incident for announcement over radio and television.

—This story ends unhappily. Write a story involving the same characters (king, people of the court, boy in the kitchen) and the same problem (that there is too much noise), but that has a happy ending.

—Draw a picture of the king, arm outstretched and pointing, as he orders the guards to close the doors.

—'How to be a good king' – five important rules.

—There is a short scene in Shakespeare's *Julius Caesar* (Act 3 Scene 3) which gives another example of how vicious a mob can be. In that scene, a poet is mistaken for one of the men who had killed Caesar; they are both called Cinna. If you can find some friends to help you to act it out, so much the better. Go easy with your friend playing Cinna!

Nuts and bolts

Exclamation marks

Exclamation marks, or 'shriek marks' as they are sometimes known, should be sparingly used, and never more than one at a time.

—Find two examples in our unit. How do they affect the reading aloud of the sentences concerned?

Unit 29

Escape by canoe

Four Polish children are on a hazardous journey to Switzerland during the Second World War.

The current was swift. In the darkness the great wooded hills swept by. For a moment the moon peeped from a cloud and turned the rippling surface of the stream to silver.

'Stay away, moon,' Ruth muttered. 'Don't come out again till we've passed the village.'

Side by side, the two canoes sped on.

On the left bank the line of the hills curved downwards. Were those dim shapes houses? Had they reached the village?

Again the moon appeared. It had chosen quite the wrong moment, for this was indeed the village, with houses crowded about both banks, and on the left bank suddenly an open space with lorries in it. They were so close together that they were almost touching, and there were several rows of them. These must be the lorries that were to take the Polish refugees back to Poland. With a tightening of fear in her throat, Ruth realised that if they were spotted now, they would be taken back too.

'Look out for the bridge,' said Edek.

He and Jan shot ahead, aiming for the centre of the three arches. Edging away from the square, Ruth paddled towards the right-hand arch.

Edek's canoe shot under the arch and disappeared into the shadows. Too far to the right, Ruth got caught in sluggish water. She drifted broadside on to the the base of the arch. She paddled frantically to get free, but the canoe was still across the base of the arch, with the water thrusting against each end, threatening to break

its back. She jabbed hard with the paddle and managed to ease it a little.

With a last effort she thrust at the stonework, and the canoe broke free. The canoe swung sideways into the shadows under the arch, then shot out beyond the bridge.

Ruth peered ahead to see if she could see anything of the other canoe.

Then the moon went behind a cloud, and the darkness hid her.

On and on they sped, the water foaming against the bows, spitting and bubbling against the canvas.

'I'm sitting in the river,' said Bronia.

But Ruth took no notice. 'Edek! Jan!' she shouted.

As they rounded a bend, they were thrust towards the right bank. The river was quieter here, and soon they felt the bottom of the canoe scrape over pebbles and slow them to a halt.

Ruth put her hand over the side and down into the water and tried to shove them off. But they were stuck. There was a pale light in the sky now, and the rim of the hills stood out dark against it. It was still too dark to see much, but she could make out rocks in the water, rounded like hippos' backs.

'We'll have to get out and push,' she said.

They stepped into the water, which was little more than ankle-deep, and at once the canoe floated. With the painter in her hand and Bronia beside her, she drew it gently along till they came to a large V-shaped rock that seemed to project from the bank. She pulled the canoe high and dry on to a shoal of pebbles, then lifted Bronia on to the rock.

'We must wait here till daylight,' she said.

And they sat there shivering and clinging to each other till the shadows brightened and they could see the whole sweep of the river, white and broken in the middle, rock-strewn and shallow at either side, with the wood-muffled hills hemming it in, and not a soul in sight. No sign of Edek and Jan. They could not have felt lonelier.

They turned the canoe over and poured water out. Stepping aboard, they headed for mid-stream. And the current caught them and carried them on towards the rapids.

The river grew faster, and the bank flashed past. Soon they were in a kind of gorge, where the river squeezed past great boulders, some of them as high as houses. Some of the swells were over a foot high, and the spray dashed over the bow and stung their faces. The water roared here so that even the loudest shout could not be heard. Out to the left there were huge oily surges that looked as if they would pound you down into the depths if you got caught in them.

Bronia closed her eyes and clung to her sister's waist. Ruth was not as scared as she had expected to be. With a triumphant sense of exhilaration she flashed in with her paddle, heading always for the open stream, away from the white broken water where the rocks lay hidden. Now and then a boulder loomed up, and she knew that if they struck it they would be dashed to pieces. But a quick dip of the paddle at the right moment was enough to shoot them safely past.

In no time the river broadened, the boulders eased, and the banks were wooded again. The terrors of the rapids were over. Ruth hoped that Edek and Jan, whose two-seater was much less easy to manoeuvre, had been as successful as they had.

There seemed no need for the paddle now, for the water was clear of rocks and the current smooth and swift. They could lie back and let the canoe take care of itself.

Bronia closed her eyes and fell asleep. Ruth lay back and watched the blue sky overhead and the climbing sun. It was to be another scorching day, and she too became sleepy and dozed.

The Silver Sword: Ian Serraillier

Comment

Ruth, Bronia and Edek are two sisters and a brother of a family searching for their parents; Jan, not related to them, is a remarkable lad who is instrumental in helping the family to come together. The story, based firmly on actual experience, shifts between the excitement of escape and the fear of being caught. There are moments when all seems to be lost, but the children's resilience and courage makes them win through.

This episode captures the exhilaration felt as they shoot down the river in canoes. They want the light of the moon to see the course of the river, but not when the river passes through villages and towns, as there is more risk of being spotted: children in canoes in wartime would arouse suspicion, and the lorries for transporting Polish refugees seem uncomfortably close.

Activities

– Continue from where this extract finishes, with Ruth and Bronia dozing in the sunlight. Remember they have lost sight of the canoe in which Jan and Edek are paddling.
– Have you ever been in a canoe? If so, write about your experiences. What was your most exciting moment and/or your most difficult? What advice would you give to someone about to begin canoeing?
– Find a map of Central Europe in an atlas, and see how far the children had to travel; they began their journey in Warsaw and were re-united with their parents in Switzerland.
– After the war a children's village was established for refugee children from all over Europe; the parents of Ruth, Bronia and Edek looked after several orphaned children from Poland. Find out about Pestalozzi and the Pestalozzi villages, asking a librarian or teacher to help, if necessary.
– If you had to leave home in a hurry (in ten minutes, say, because of a flood warning) with only a small rucksack, what items would you include and why? Ask a friend or a member of your family what he or she would take, and compare lists.
– *The Silver Sword* is a gripping story. Read how the children's father, a headmaster, escaped from a prison camp; how Edek caused their house to be blown up; and how Edek became an icicle! Another journey of a similar nature, but more contemporary, is narrated in Anne Holm's book, *I am David*.

Nuts and bolts

Sentences

About half-way through the unit you will see a sentence beginning 'With the painter in her hand'. Read it. Notice how it is built up on the basic sentence 'she drew it gently along' and see how these additions are made, one at a time:

With the painter in her hand and Bronia beside her till they came to a large V-shaped rock that seemed to project from the bank
– About a quarter of the way through, find the sentence beginning 'With a tightening of fear . . .' and in the same way see how it is built up.

Unit 30

Pip and the convict

Pip thinks he is alone in the churchyard where his parents are buried.

'Hold your noise!' cried a terrible voice, as a man started up from among the graves at the side of the church porch. 'Keep still, you little devil, or I'll cut your throat!'

A fearful man, all in coarse grey, with a great iron on his leg. A man with no hat, and with broken shoes, and with an old rag tied round his head. A man who had been soaked in water, and smothered in mud, and lamed by stones, and cut by flints, and stung by nettles, and torn by briars; who limped, and shivered, and glared and growled; and whose teeth chattered in his head as he seized me by the chin.

'O! Don't cut my throat, sir.' I pleaded in terror. 'Pray don't do it, sir.'

'Tell us your name!' said the man. 'Quick!'

'Pip, sir.'

'Once more,' said the man, staring at me. 'Give it mouth!'

'Pip. Pip, sir.'

'Show us where you live,' said the man. 'Pint out the place!'

I pointed to where our village lay, on the flat in-shore among the alder trees and pollards, a mile or more from the church.

The man, after looking at me for a moment, turned me upside down, and emptied my pockets. There was nothing in them but a piece of bread. When the church came to itself – for he was so sudden and strong that he made it go head over heels before me, and I saw the steeple under my feet – when the church came to itself, I say, I was seated on a high tombstone, trembling, while he ate the bread ravenously.

'You young dog,' said the man, licking his lips, 'what fat cheeks you ha' got.'

I believe they were fat, though I was at that time undersized for my years, and not strong.

'Darn me if I couldn't eat 'em,' said the man, with a threatening shake of his head, 'and if I han't half a mind to 't!'

I earnestly expressed my hope that he wouldn't, and held tighter to the tombstone on which he had put me; partly, to keep myself upon it; partly, to keep myself from crying.

'Now lookee here!' said the man. 'Where's your mother?'

'There, sir!' said I.

He started, made a short run, and stopped and looked over his shoulder.

'There, sir!' I timidly explained. 'Also Georgiana. That's my mother.'

'Oh!' said he, coming back. 'And is that your father alonger your mother?'

'Yes, sir,' said I; 'him too; late of this parish.'

'Ha!' he muttered then, considering. 'Who d'ye

live with – supposin' you're kindly let to live, which I han't made up my mind about?'

'My sister, sir – Mrs Joe Gargery – wife of Joe Gargery, the blacksmith, sir.'

'Blacksmith, eh?' said he. And looked down at his leg.

After darkly looking at his leg and me several times, he came closer to my tombstone, took me by both arms, and tilted me back as far as he could hold me; so that his eyes looked most powerfully down into mine, and mine looked most helplessly up into his.

'Now lookee here,' he said, 'the question being whether you're to be let to live. You know what a file is?'

'Yes, sir.'

'And you know what wittles is?'

'Yes, sir.'

After each question he tilted me over a little more, so as to give me a greater sense of helplessness and danger.

'You get me a file.' He tilted me again. 'And you get me wittles.' He tilted me again. 'You bring 'em both to me.' He tilted me again. 'Or I'll have your heart and liver out.' He tilted me again.

Great Expectations: Charles Dickens

Comment

In the second paragraph of this extract Dickens describes the escaping convict most carefully; he is a terrifying figure to young Pip. But, by describing the rough conditions the convict has endured with a great iron on his leg (to mark him out as a convict and to make movement difficult), Dickens forces us to look at him with some sympathy.

The man's gruff voice and short snappy statements and questions help us feel his agitation. Dickens gives a clue to his accent by making him pronounce 'point' as 'pint', 'victuals' (a word meaning food and normally pronounced 'vittles') as 'wittles', and by clipping words – 'em, 't, han't.

Activities

– Describe Pip's journey home after the convict released him, thinking back over his horrible experience and wondering how to acquire the file and some food without arousing the suspicions of his sister and brother-in-law.

– The return. Imagine Pip's journey back to the churchyard to deliver the file and food.

– Write about the convict's last twenty-four hours before he met Pip. You could include his escape.

– If you were Pip, would you decide to return with the convict's requests or would you go to the police?

– The extract begins abruptly. We have given you only one sentence to lead you into the story. If you had to make a film, how would you begin, so that an atmosphere was created and established before the convict appeared? Draw a plan of the churchyard and surrounding countryside and indicate where you would place your cameras. What sound effects or music, if any, would you use?

– Find out what happened to Pip and the convict by reading the novel from which this extract is taken. This extract is early in the first chapter.

Nuts and bolts

Paragraphs

In a well-written paragraph every sentence fits into place, coming naturally after what has just been written. There is often a link between one sentence and another, such as: But . . . As a result . . . After that . . . This action . . . etc. Similarly paragraphs are often linked with their neighbours before and after; a paragraph for instance may end with a hint that a fresh point is coming, or it may start by referring back to the previous paragraph.

– Look at the second paragraph of our unit. Everything is linked to the first sentence by 'A man with . . .' 'A man who . . .' 'and whose teeth . . .'

– Read the first paragraph of Comment and look carefully to see the links there.

Unit 31

Adolf

Father has brought home a little wild rabbit:

By evening the little creature was tame, quite tame. He was christened Adolf. We were enchanted by him. We couldn't really love him, because he was wild and loveless to the end. But he was an unmixed delight.

We decided he was too small to live in a hutch – he must live at large in the house. My mother protested, but in vain. He was so tiny. So we had him upstairs, and he dropped his tiny pills on the bed and we were enchanted.

Adolf made himself instantly at home. He had the run of the house, and was perfectly happy, with his tunnels and holes behind the furniture.

We loved him to take meals with us. He would sit on the table humping his back, hopping off and hobbling back to his saucer, with an air of supreme unconcern. Suddenly he was alert. He hobbled a few tiny paces, and reared himself up inquisitively at the sugar basin. He fluttered his tiny forepaws, and then reached and laid them on the edge of the basin, whilst he craned his thin neck and peeped in. He trembled his whiskers at the sugar, then did his best to lift down a lump.

'*Do* you think I will have it! Animals in the sugar-pot!' cried my mother, with a rap of her hand on the table. Which so delighted the electric Adolf that he flung his hindquarters and knocked over a cup.

One day between them they overturned the cream-jug. Adolf deluged his little chest, bounced back in terror, was seized by his little ears by my mother and bounced down on the hearthrug. There he shivered in momentary discomfort, and suddenly set off on a wild flight to the parlour.

This last was his happy hunting ground. He had cultivated the bad habit of pensively nibbling certain bits of cloth in the hearthrug. When chased from this pasture he would retreat under the sofa. There he would twinkle in Buddhist meditation until suddenly, no one knew why, he would go off like an alarm clock. With a sudden bumping scuffle he would whirl out of the room, going through the doorway with his little ears flying. Then we would hear his thunderbolt hurtling in the parlour, but before we could follow, the wild streak of Adolf would flash past us, on an electric wind that carried him round the scullery and carried him back, a little mad thing, flying possessed like a ball round the parlour. After which he would sit in a corner composed and distant, twitching his whiskers in abstract meditation.

One day, as we were playing by the stile, I saw his brown shadow loiter across the road and pass into the field that faced the houses. Instantly a cry of 'Adolf!' – a cry that he knew full well. And instantly a wind swept him away down the sloping meadow, his tail twinkling and zigzagging through the grass. After him we pelted. It was a strange sight to see him, ears back, his little loins so powerful, flinging the world behind him. We ran ourselves out of breath, but could not catch him. Then somebody headed him off, and he sat with sudden unconcern, twitching his nose under a bunch of nettles.

Adolf was becoming too much for mother. He dropped too many pills. And suddenly to hear him clumping downstairs when she was alone in the house was startling. And to keep him from the door was impossible. Cats prowled outside. It was worse than having a child to look after.

Yet we would not have him shut up. He became more lusty, more callous than ever. He was a strong kicker, and many a scratch on face and arms did we owe to him. But he brought his own doom on himself. The lace curtains in the parlour – my mother was rather proud of them – fell on the floor very full. One of Adolf's joys was to scuffle wildly through them as though some foamy undergrowth. He had already torn rents in them.

One day he entangled himself altogether. He kicked, he whirled round in a mad nebulous inferno. He screamed – and brought the curtain-rod with a smash, right on the best beloved pelargonium, just as my mother rushed in. She extricated him, but she never forgave him. And he never forgave either. A heartless wildness had come over him.

Even we understood that he must go. It was decided, after a long deliberation, that my father should carry him back to the wild-woods. Once again he was stowed into the great pocket of the pit-jacket.

'Best pop him i' th' pot,' said my father, who enjoyed raising the wind of indignation.

And so, the next day, our father said that Adolf, set down on the edge of the coppice, had hopped away with utmost indifference, neither elated nor moved. We heard it and believed. But many, many were the heart-searchings. How would the other rabbits receive him? Would they smell his tameness, his humanised degradation, and rend him? My mother pooh-poohed the extravagant idea.

Phoenix: D.H. Lawrence

Comment

We know what it is like to keep a wild young animal in the house; and we also learn a bit about the parents. Father liked bringing home something that would please his children, and liked teasing them, but otherwise he did not bother himself much. Mother is very tolerant; she seems to have put up with more than some mothers would.

Later on the father said that early in the morning on his way to work he had seen Adolf and had called him, but in vain. His son would go to the edge of the coppice and call softly, and would imagine he saw bright eyes between the nettle stalks.

The poet William Cowper kept a hare called Tiney in his house for eight years, but it was always wild, surly and ready to bite. It grew more courageous in the evening, its main time for skipping and bounding about the place.

Activities

– Adolf sounds rather a character, behaving in ways we think of as human. Note down his human-like qualities.

– Imagine a conversation between the mother and a neighbour about the new family 'pet'.

– The writer says that Adolf hopped away when the father let him go. He then asks 'How would the other rabbits receive him?' Write a story entitled 'The Homecoming' as if you were Adolf or one of his relatives. You will find this easier to do if you have read *Watership Down* by Richard Adams, a book we recommended in Unit 9, *Practice makes perfect.*

– If you keep an animal of any kind, write some notes for the benefit of a friend who is thinking of keeping one. You should make the notes under certain headings: cost, room/cage, feeding, cleaning, snags, keeping the pet healthy – for example.

– In the Comment we referred to William Cowper. His poem 'Epitaph on a Hare' and an account of his tame hares can be found in *Voices* (First Book), edited by Geoffrey Summerfield.

Nuts and bolts

Expansion from notes

When you are making notes for something which later on is going to be written up at length, it will be best to make fairly full notes, clearly arranged. For example, if you are going to make notes for writing or speaking about keeping a pet animal, your notes might go something like this:

1 **Where to get the animal**

What sort of dealer
Points to look for —
cautions

2 **Accommodation for it, in**

Winter
Summer
Breeding season

3 **Food**

Varied diet
Examples
Where to get it
Drink

4 **Care**

Keeping it well
Diseases
How to treat them

5 **Summary**

Why it is enjoyable

– For practice, make notes and write them up on one of these topics: A present you would like; a place you would like to go to; a new subject or activity you would like introduced into school; the holiday you would like to go on.

Unit 32

The retired artist

Tom Sawyer's aunt gives him a job as a punishment for tearing his clothes. He dreads the jeers of his friends:

At this dark and hopeless moment an inspiration burst upon him. He took up his brush and went tranquilly to work. Ben Rogers hove in sight presently; the very boy whose ridicule he had been dreading.

He was eating an apple, and giving a long melodious whoop at intervals, followed by a deep-toned, ding, dong, dong, for he was personating a steamboat! As he drew near he slackened speed, took the middle of the street, and rounded-to ponderously, for he was personating the *Big Missouri*, and considered himself to be drawing nine feet of water. He was boat, and captain, and engine bells combined, so he had to imagine himself standing on his own hurricane-deck giving the orders and executing them.

'Stop her, sir! Ling-a-ling-ling.' He drew up slowly towards the side-walk. 'Set her back on the stabbord! Ling-a-ling-ling! Chow! ch-chow-wow-chow!' his right hand meanwhile describing stately circles, for it was representing a forty-foot wheel.

Tom went on whitewashing – paid no attention to the steamer. Ben stared a moment, and then said:

'Hi-yi! You're up a stump, ain't you?'

'Why, it's you, Ben! I warn't noticing.'

'Say, I'm going in a swimming, I am. Don't you wish you could? But of course you'd druther work, wouldn't you? 'Course you would!'

Tom contemplated the boy a bit, and said:

'What do you call work?'

'Why, ain't that work?'

Tom resumed his whitewashing, and answered carelessly:

'Well, maybe it is, and maybe it ain't. All I know is, it suits Tom Sawyer.'

'Oh, come now, you don't mean to let on that you like it?'

The brush continued to move.

'Like it? Why, I don't see why I oughtn't to like it. Does a boy get a chance to whitewash a fence every day?'

That put the thing in a new light. Ben stopped nibbling his apple. Tom swept his brush daintily back and forth – stepping back to note the effect – added a touch here and there – criticised the effect again, Ben watching every move, and getting more and more interested, more and more absorbed. Presently he said:

'Say, Tom, let me whitewash a little.'

Tom considered; was about to consent; but he altered his mind: 'No, no, I reckon it wouldn't hardly do, Ben. You see, Aunt Polly's awful particular about this fence – right here on the street, you know – but if it was the back fence I wouldn't mind, and she wouldn't. I reckon there ain't one boy in a thousand, maybe two thousand, that can do it the way it's got to be done.'

'No, is that so? Oh, come now, lemme just try, only a little. I'd let you, if you was me, Tom.'

The steamboat *Cochan* on the Colorado River, in the 1890s.

'Ben, I'd like to, honest injun; but Aunt Polly – well, Jim wanted to do it, but she wouldn't let him. Sid wanted to do it, but she wouldn't let Sid. Now, don't you see how I'm fixed? If you was to tackle this fence, and anything was to happen to it –'

'Oh, shucks; I'll be just as careful. Now lemme try. Say – I'll give the core of my apple.'

'Well, here. No Ben; now don't; I'm afeard –'

'I'll give you all of it!'

Tom gave up the brush with reluctance in his face but alacrity in his heart. And while the late steamer *Big Missouri* worked and sweated in the sun, the retired artist sat on a barrel in the shade close by, dangled his legs, munched his apple, and planned the slaughter of more innocents. There was no lack of material: boys happened along every little while; they came to jeer, but remained to whitewash. By the time Ben was fagged out, Tom had traded the next chance to Billy Fisher for a kite in good repair; and when he played out, Johnny Miller bought in for a dead rat and a string to swing it with; and so on, and so on, hour after hour. And when the middle of the afternoon came, from being a poor poverty-stricken boy in the morning Tom was literally rolling in wealth. He had, besides the things I have mentioned, twelve marbles, part of a jew's harp, a piece of blue bottle-glass to look through, a spool-cannon, a key that wouldn't unlock anything, a fragment of chalk, a glass stopper of a decanter, a kitten with only one eye, a brass door-knob, a dog collar – but no dog – the handle of a knife, four pieces of orange peel, and a dilapidated old window-sash. He had had a nice, good, idle time all the while – plenty of company – and the fence had three coats of whitewash on it! If he hadn't run out of whitewash he would have bankrupted every boy in the village.

The Adventures of Tom Sawyer: Mark Twain

Comment

This comes from the story of Tom Sawyer's escapades with the truant Huck Finn and Jim, the runaway slave. Twain himself ran away from home to become a cub pilot (apprentice) on one of the big paddle steamers that risked the currents, snags and shoals of the ever-changing Mississippi; and it was about life on the river and its banks that he wrote his splendid books.

Our extract shows that something special or demanding skill and endurance (like breaking records and climbing Everest) will always attract men and women. There are many strenuous jobs, like playing in an orchestra, that are a livelihood to some people and a hobby to others. We like the piece because Twain is so good at getting right inside his characters; we understand just what they felt and why they acted as they did.

Activities

– 'The day I conned my friends': write a similar story to Mark Twain's. It might be about an experience you have had.

– Invent another episode involving Tom and his friends Ben Rogers, Billy Fisher, and Johnny Miller. You can bring in Tom's Aunt Polly if you wish.

– Tom gains a range of objects from his friends that both they and he find valuable. What 'treasures' did you have when you were younger? Do you still have some? Write about why you value them. For the memories associated with them, their beauty?

– Think of three occupations that can be either work or pleasure, according to whether they are paid or not, and say what is attractive about them. If you are stuck, think of railways, horses, aircraft.

– Read *Huckleberry Finn, Tom Sawyer* or *Life on the Mississippi*, Twain's own account of his apprenticeship. If you find the American dialect difficult, read *The Prince and the Pauper*, which tells how Tom Conty and Prince Edward exchanged their lives and identity. It is good reading.

Nuts and bolts

Hyphens

Hyphens are like railway couplings. They link words together: deep-toned, hurricane-deck. When a pair of hyphenated words have been together a long time, the hyphen tends to be dropped: steamboat, whitewash.

– Find some linking hyphens in the unit.

Hyphens are also used when a word is broken in two, to allow it to be finished in the next line of print. In this book the lines are *unjustified*. This means that the lines do not have to be exactly the same length, with words broken to fit.

Unit 33

Dolls

When you peer into a toy-shop window and see a doll, carefully packaged and waiting for an owner, you are probably unaware that you are looking at an idea that has existed for centuries. For the making of dolls is a very, very old custom.

Archaeologists have found evidence of dolls in ancient Greek and Roman remains. Indeed, there is a little Roman rag doll, dating from AD 4, in the British Museum in London which comes from a child's grave.

Playing with dolls is customarily associated with girls, but there are many boys, as well as girls who have teddy bears. The late poet laureate, Sir John Betjeman, kept his teddy bear right until his death. And should you be tempted to think it is only girls that play with dolls, what about Action Man with his many available outfits and equipment?

Japanese boys enjoy similar fun with toy images of warriors. They even have an annual festival at which these images are displayed. The girls, not to be outdone, have their own festival too; but their dolls are more to do with having children.

Dolls are universal; there are few countries without some tradition of dolls. The American Indians endowed their wooden images with sacred properties; the Hindus and Moslems gave elaborately dressed dolls as wedding presents; in parts of Africa, when a girl becomes of age, she is given a doll which she keeps until she has a child, her mother giving her another doll until a second is born, and so on.

In Christian Europe small figures have been used as images of saints and, most importantly, have been associated with the Christmas crib.

In the interests of modesty, Chinese ladies owned little naked dolls made out of ivory to show doctors where they felt aches and pains, there being no need therefore to point to parts of their own bodies! Apparently this practice continued up until last century.

To find out the latest fashions of the French Court – before the days of illustrations – dolls dressed in the most fashionable clothes would be sent to other countries for the dressmakers to copy. Having served their purpose, the dolls would then be given to the daughters to play with.

French dolls were famous at the time of the French Revolution for a purpose somewhat different from that of fashion. Dolls with detachable heads, and used in conjunction with toy guillotines, provided a bloodthirsty pastime for the young.

There is a famous story of a doll-maker whose wife was so grief-stricken at the death of their daughter that she became seriously ill, no one being able to console her. The doll-maker himself found difficulty in concentrating on his work; he missed his daughter and he was anxious for his wife's health. One day he sat whittling a piece of wood when he discovered that the face of the angel he was carving was taking on the features of his daughter. Having finished the angel, he placed it at his wife's bedside so that she would see it immediately on waking. His wife was so pleased that her health gradually improved. The doll-maker found so much joy in making replicas of his daughter that he devoted the rest of his life to making and selling them.

Over the centuries, dolls have been made from, and stuffed with, every kind of material, from grass to porcelain, sawdust to feathers; the clothes peg wrapped in a handkerchief has been popular with many children. The so-called 'rag' doll, the doll made from whatever scraps of material are at hand, has its own individuality and interest. In *Doll Making – A Creative Approach*, Jean Ray Laury writes: 'The best-loved dolls of children are those which provide some basis on which the imagination can feed. If everything is there (the doll that walks, talks, wets, cries, and sleeps), what is left but the mechanical manipulation of these machined parts? It is the child who should give life to the doll, not the reverse. Children assume that dolls have human responses – they seem to realise that it is they who animate the dolls, and breathe into them the qualities they recognise or comprehend and embrace. The rag doll, the cuddly doll, is the one that can hugged, slept with, retrieved after a few days of neglect, and still remain 'intact' after all this. China dolls, or the old wax dolls, were intimidating and therefore less loved. More admired, perhaps, and highly prized, but less loved. Plastic and composition dolls are not quite so forbidding as china ones, but a child cannot put such a doll beneath her head and sleep comfortably on it. Any time a child is admonished by a mother that she'll 'get the doll dirty' or 'ruin its hair', that doll does not belong to the child. And few first possessions are more loved or longer remembered than dolls.'

An English wax doll with stuffed linen body wearing the kind of dress worn by a girl of sixteen in 1858

An English wax doll, dating from about 1850, with a carved wooden body and eyes that open and close. Originally owned by a daughter of Queen Victoria.

A Roman doll in the form of a soldier

Unit 33 continued

Comment

Making models of humans is an art shared by dollmakers and sculptors alike, going back over the centuries and over very many countries. This article gives some interesting, and probably surprising, information.

The last paragraph points to important reasons for the popularity which dolls have enjoyed: first, dolls can be made from almost anything; they don't have to be expensive. And secondly, the child develops his or her imagination by giving life and personality to a doll. Dolls give security and comfort, but also (if you have ever watched a young child playing, you will have noticed) dolls have to do as they are told and get smacked if they disobey!

Left
An English wax doll with a cloth body, dating from 1853 and thought to represent Queen Victoria's daughter, Princess Louise as a baby.

Below left
A French doll with a jointed composition body, dating from about 1890

Activities

(N.B. In these activities we have used the word 'doll' to mean any model in human form. It could mean, for example, the model of an old man bent over his walking stick.)
– Several books about making dolls are available, most libraries probably having one or two. Gain some ideas, then make up a doll from whatever material you can find. You could give it to a younger brother or sister, cousin, friend, or you could offer to make several for a sale.
– A doll comes to life. Make up a story suitable for reading to a young child (a four-year-old, say). You could combine this with the previous activity, making the story about the doll you have made. It helps if you have a particular child in mind as you write.
– 'Playing with dolls is a waste of time and effort,' says a friend of yours, on seeing your collection of bits of material, wool, pipe cleaners, etc., prior to your making a doll. Give your friend two examples of when dolls served practical purposes.
– Did you have a favourite toy when you were younger, not necessarily a doll? Write a paragraph about it.

Action Man

—If possible, go to see the Bethnal Green Museum of Childhood, Cambridge Heath Road, London, E2. In a newspaper article about the museum it was stated that 'Students of the history of doll-making could spend days studying the range and different techniques used, which are all well documented; and visitors of any age would find much enjoyment in looking at what our forebears collected or played with.'

You will also find other collections in other parts of the country. The local tourist board would no doubt help you.

—For research: look up *Coppélia, Pinocchio, Petrushka* and find out their connection with this unit.

Nuts and bolts

Note-making

All sorts of people need to make notes, such as scientists watching an experiment, or apprentices studying a handbook about the job they are learning. You yourself will have to make notes, perhaps about a hobby or in preparing for a class discussion.

—Try splitting up this article on dolls with 'cross-headings' (the little headings inserted between paragraphs by journalists); each cross-heading will be a note or two on the paragraph or two following.

Unit 34

Teachers for a month

The teacher of a little village school is away and the children continue running the school on their own. Ruth and Shirley do the teaching, and then Miss Oldroyd returns. Just in time, because the two young teachers could not be expected to go on any longer:

Everybody stood up. Miss Oldroyd stepped into the room, and looked about. Ruth wished the school had been perfectly tidy, without any dust, and with the board clean. Shirley came away from the teacher's desk and closed the book she had been reading from. 'What are you doing here?' said Miss Oldroyd. 'I thought you had all gone to Burton school.'

No one said anything. Shirley looked at Ruth. Ruth looked at the rest of the class, and then at Miss Oldroyd.

'Haven't you been to Burton school at all?' said Miss Oldroyd.

'No,' said Fletcher. 'It's a spot and all.'

'Did Mrs Tunstall come down here, then?' said Miss Oldroyd. 'Where is she now?'

Ruth put her fingers in the belt of her dress and twisted it. 'We did it ourselves,' she said. 'I taught some days.' She was not going to let Shirley be blamed.

'And I taught the other days,' said Shirley. 'I was teaching now.'

'They were so quiet,' said Miss Oldroyd. 'I thought the school was empty. I was taken aback you know, when I saw you all here. I only came to get some books and see about Monday's lessons. But I don't think you really need me, do you? Can I go away for another month?'

'We thought it would be all right,' said Ruth. 'It was my fault, I thought of it, and I made them come.' She was not sure yet whether they were going to get into trouble for what she had led them to do. Miss Oldroyd had only been talking, without saying so far what she felt. Ruth felt something like crying beginning to make a lump in her throat and prickle behind her eyes. She twisted her fingers very tight in her belt.

'I think you've done very well,' said Miss Oldroyd. 'I see you've even got some new pupils, too.'

The lump in Ruth's throat grew very big indeed, and her eyes suddenly grew very hot. It was because hot tears were filling them. The hot tears began to run down her face, and the lump in her

throat melted into a sob. She tried to keep her face straight, but it wrinkled up; and then she was crying properly.

'I sometimes feel like that on a Friday too,' said Miss Oldroyd. 'I generally feel better after I've given our Fletcher a crack, and Bobby and Peter too, as often as not.'

'They've been very good,' said Ruth. 'They made the best dinner we ever had.' She meant to say it in a very calm sort of way, but the words were all tangled with sobs, so that they all came squeaky and jumpy.

'Dinners too,' said Miss Oldroyd. 'Have you made the dinners too?'

'You were away, so Mary Crofts didn't come,' said Shirley. 'She wouldn't, would she?'

'Not if she didn't know,' said Miss Oldroyd. 'There now, Ruth, sit down and have your cry comfortably, and the rest can go out for a playtime. Is that all right, teacher?'

'Yes,' said Shirley. 'It's about time.'

'Anybody else want a good cry?' said Miss Oldroyd. 'Because I think I'm going to have one.'

'I've got one, but it won't come,' said Shirley.

'Stay and talk to us,' said Miss Oldroyd. She sat down beside Ruth and took out her handkerchief. First she mopped up Ruth's tears. Ruth smelt the scent on the handkerchief, faint and sweet. Then Miss Oldroyd dabbed her own eyes. 'I can't help it,' she said. 'You poor things, taking on a whole school by yourselves. Tell me about everything.'

Ruth picked up her skirt and dried her face on it. Her eyes were feeling much cooler now, and the tears were drying, and the sobs were only coming into her chest and not up into her face.

'We haven't been polite yet,' she said. 'How are you, Miss Oldroyd?'

'I'm very well now, thank you,' said Miss Oldroyd. 'I had a lovely rest, and I'm ready to start again on Monday.'

'Oh, good,' said Ruth. 'I'm glad you're well.'

'We don't mind teaching,' said Shirley. 'But the cooking goes on and on. That's why we let the boys do it.'

'Tell me,' said Miss Oldroyd.

They told her about everything; how they had forgotten about dinner on the first day; how the filter had been left running after the telephone had frightened them; how they thought an inspector had come; how Fletcher had been naughty and how he had got his good name back again; how they had filled in the card for the sports and practised; how they had taught Bill and Susan their writing.

No More School: William Mayne

Comment

This piece makes us feel as if we were there, taking part in the scene on the return of Miss Oldroyd. It is all so true to life; we know just what was going on in Ruth's mind. First she is very worried that they may have done wrong in carrying on as they did; and then, when she realizes that Miss Oldroyd is actually pleased, she breaks down. We sympathize with her crying; we look at things through her eyes and we feel what she feels. So that we are entirely on her side. Where in the piece do we first learn that Miss Oldroyd approved? And did you notice the places which tell us how nervous Ruth was?

Activities

– Your teacher fails to turn up for a lesson. Rather than inform the school office, you decide to organize yourselves. Describe the argument and what happens in the lesson.
– If you have a favourite subject, describe the lesson you most enjoyed.
– Jot down a list of the qualities you think a good teacher ought to have.
– The paragraph beginning 'The lump in Ruth's throat grew very big indeed' describes vividly how Ruth began to cry. Have you ever felt like that? What happened?
– You are a journalist who has heard of the girls' attempts as teachers. Make up a suitable headline and write a newspaper article.
– *The Whole Truth*, a play by Ray Jenkins, is about a class left by themselves to organize a court in a drama lesson. It's well worth reading.

Nuts and bolts

Spelling

Some groups of words have family likenesses: brick, thick, stick, lick. In some words the resemblance is at the end: bargain, captain, curtain, fountain, mountain. We find it a help with some of our own spelling problems to make up jingly nonsense rhymes to fix the words in the mind. So for the family just mentioned:

Captain Fountain said that the shop on the mountain had bargains in curtains.

Another family consists of words containing the letters 'gh', though they make no sound at all: 'taught' and 'eight', for examples.
– Look through the unit and find four more members of this family.

Unit 35

Life at Dotheboys Hall

Mr Squeers runs a notorious school. Nicholas Nickleby, his new assistant, sits down to wait for the school to start:

He could not but observe how silent and sad the boys all seemed to be. There was none of the noise and clamour of a schoolroom; none of its boisterous play, or hearty mirth. The children sat crouching and shivering together, and seemed to lack the spirit to move about. The only pupil who evinced the slightest tendency towards locomotion or playfulness was Master Squeers, and as his chief amusement was to tread upon the other boys' toes in his new boots, his flow of spirits was rather disagreeable than otherwise.

After some half-hour's delay, Mr Squeers reappeared, and the boys took their places and their books, of which latter commodity the average might be about one to eight learners. A few minutes having elapsed, during which Mr Squeers looked very profound, as if he had a perfect apprehension of what was inside all the books and could say every word of their contents by heart if he only chose to take the trouble, that gentleman called up the first class.

Obedient to this summons there ranged themselves in front of the schoolmaster's desk, half a dozen scarecrows, out at knees and elbows, one of whom placed a torn and filthy book beneath his Learned eye.

'This is the first class in English spelling and philosophy, Nickleby,' said Squeers, beckoning Nicholas to stand beside him. 'We'll get up a Latin one, and hand that over to you. Now, then, where's the first boy?'

'Please, sir, he's cleaning the back parlour window,' said the temporary head of the philosophical class.

'So he is, to be sure,' rejoined Squeers. 'We go upon the practical mode of teaching, Nickleby; the regular education system. C-l-e-a-n, clean, verb active, to make bright, to scour. W-i-n, win, d-e-r, der, winder, a casement. When the boy knows this out of the book, he goes and does it. It's just the same principle as the use of the globes. Where's the second boy?'

'Please, sir, he's weeding the garden,' replied a small voice.

'To be sure,' said Squeers, by no means disconcerted. 'So he is. B-o-t, bot, t-i-n, bottin, n-e-y, bottinney, noun substantive, a knowledge of plants. When he has learned that bottinney means a knowledge of plants, he goes and knows 'em. That's our system, Nickleby; what do you think of it?'

'It's a very useful one, at any rate,' answered Nicholas.

'I believe you,' rejoined Squeers, not remarking the emphasis of his usher. 'Third boy, what's a horse?'

'A beast, sir,' replied the boy.

'So it is,' said Squeers. 'Ain't it, Nickleby?'

'I believe there is no doubt of that, sir,' answered Nicholas.

'Of course there isn't,' said Squeers. 'A horse is a quadruped, and quadruped's Latin for beast, as every body that's gone through the grammar knows, or else where's the use of having grammars at all?'

'Where, indeed!' said Nicholas abstractedly.

'As you're perfect in that,' resumed Squeers, turning to the boy, 'go and look after my horse; and rub him down well, or I'll rub you down. The rest of the class go and draw water up, till somebody tells you to leave off, for it's washing-day tomorrow, and they want the coppers filled.'

So saying, he dismissed the first class to their experiments in practical philosophy, and eyed Nicholas with a look, half cunning and half doubtful, as if he were not altogether certain what he might think of him by this time.

'That's the way we do it, Nickleby,' he said, after a pause.

Nicholas shrugged his shoulders in a manner that was scarcely perceptible, and said he saw it was.

'And a very good way it is, too,' said Squeers. 'Now, just take them fourteen little boys and hear them do some reading, because, you know, you must begin to be useful. Idling about here, won't do.'

Mr Squeers said this, as if it had suddenly occurred to him, either that he must not say too much to his assistant, or that his assistant did not say enough to him in praise of the establishment. The children were arranged in a semicircle round the new master, and he was soon listening to their dull, drawling, hesitating recital of those stories of engrossing interest which are to be found in the more antiquated spelling books.

Nicholas Nickleby: Charles Dickens

Comment

We see, just as Nicholas himself sees, the deplorable state of education in Dotheboys Hall: there is a lack of teaching material; the poor boys cower in front of Squeers – not the best conditions for learning; and much of what Squeers has to pass on is incorrect – his mis-spelling of 'window' and 'botany', for a start. Can you find another error he makes?

The writer uses what we call irony to achieve his effect. By irony we understand that he says the opposite of what he really means. Two examples are in the reference to Mr Squeers and his 'Learned eye' (he obviously isn't learned) and in the final paragraph to 'those stories of engrossing interest' which, being found in 'antiquated spelling books', were probably not interesting.

Dickens has made up an interesting name for the school, Dotheboys Hall. In view of what you have read in the extract about Squeers and his 'practical philosophy' can you see why it's a good name?

Activities

– You are one of the unfortunate pupils at Dotheboys Hall. It has been a particularly bad day for you; not only has Mr Squeers been unpleasant, but his son has also been doing his utmost to get you into trouble. In sheer frustration at the unfairness you decide to write home to your parents explaining why you want them to take you away.

– The boys have become so fed up with Master Squeers, a typical bully, that they have begun to make threats, oblivious of the consequences because the situation can hardly become worse. They decide to give him a last chance by submitting to him a list of 'do's' and 'don'ts'. Compile the list.

– Imagine you are Nicholas and, after a week working in Dotheboys Hall, you decide to resign. You fear that, if you tell Mr Squeers to his face, he will possibly be violent with you, so you pack your bag and leave in the early hours when everyone is asleep. You place your letter of resignation on the table in the hall. What would you write? Remember that if you say all that you would like to say it might make Squeers take out his anger on the boys.

– Re-write this extract as a self-contained short play. You may introduce more characters and dialogue.

– *Nicholas Nickleby* has had a profound influence on many people, its publication having hastened the end of schools like Dotheboys Hall. By looking at encyclopaedias and books about Dickens, try to find out as much as you can about his attitude to such schools and to education in general.

– There are two similarities between *Nicholas Nickleby* and another novel by Dickens, *Hard Times*. Find a copy and read the first chapter or two.

Nuts and bolts

Spelling

It is a common habit of English to make a fresh word by adding on a piece at the beginning, called a prefix: *anti*septic, *sub*marine, *super*fine, *motor*way, *re*decorate. These are usually fitted on without altering the original word:

    dis + trust   = distrust
    dis + appear   = disappear
    dis + satisfy = dissatisfy
    un + natural   = unnatural
    in + active   = inactive
    re + new   = renew

– How would you explain to a learner that 'uneven' and 'unnecessary' are correctly spelled?
– Look through this unit and find words which start with: dis-, re-, and semi-.

Unit 36

Pauline learns a lesson

Pauline Fossil is chosen, at the age of twelve, to play the part of Alice in *Alice in Wonderland* in the professional theatre. Her success brings her flowers, chocolates, letters, praise, but it makes her conceited – to Winifred, the under-study's advantage:

The rule of the theatre was that a cotton wrap had to be worn over all stage dresses until just before an entrance. Nana always saw that Pauline's wrap was round her when she went on to the side of the stage, and she hung it up for her when she made her entrance. When Pauline came off after the act, or during the act, she was supposed to wrap it round her. To start with Pauline was very good at remembering it, but after a bit she thought it a bore and left it hanging where Nana had left it, and the call-boy had to bring it to her dressing-room. This went on for a day or two; then one afternoon Pauline was skipping off after the first act, when the stage manager caught hold of her.

'What about your wrap, my dear?'

'Oh, bother!' said Pauline. 'Tell the call-boy to bring it.' And she ran to her room.

The stage manager took the wrap and followed her; he knocked on her door. Nana opened it.

'Good afternoon, Miss Gutheridge. Pauline must remember her wrap. The call-boy has other things to do than run after her, and it is a rule of the management's that she wears it.'

For two or three days Pauline wore her wrap; then one afternoon she deliberately left it on the stage after the last act. A few minutes later the call-boy knocked on her door.

'Mr Barnes's compliments, Miss Fossil, and will you go back for your wrap.'

'Tell him "No",' Pauline shouted. 'I'm busy.'

'Pauline,' Nana said, 'go at once when the stage manager sends for you.'

Winifred was still in the theatre. 'Let me go,' she said, jumping up.

'Sit down, Winifred.' Nana's voice was quiet. 'Either Pauline fetches it herself, or it hangs where it is.'

'Let it hang, then.'

After a few minutes there was another knock on the door. This time it was Mr Barnes.

'Did Pauline get my message?' he asked Nana.

Pauline pushed Nana to one side and came out.

'I did, and I said I wouldn't fetch it, so please stop bothering.'

Mr French, who was the managing director of the Princess Theatres, Ltd, came out of the 'Mad Hatter's' dressing-room, which was next door. He stopped in surprise.

'What's all the trouble?'

Mr Barnes looked worried, as he hated telling tales. But Nana thought a scolding would be the best thing in the world for Pauline. She told him the whole story. Mr French looked down at Pauline.

'Go and fetch your wrap at once. I don't make rules in my theatre for little girls to break.'

Pauline was excited and angry, and she completely lost her temper. She behaved as she had never behaved before. She stamped her foot.

'Get it yourselves if you want it fetched.'

There was a long pause, and in the silence Pauline began to feel frightened. Mr French was a terribly important man, and nobody was ever rude to him. His face expressed nothing, but she could feel he was angry. At last he looked at Mr Barnes.

'Is the under-study in the theatre?'

Nana called Winifred, who came out looking very nervous, for she had heard all that had gone on.

'You will play tomorrow,' Mr French said to her, 'Pauline will be in the theatre as your under-study.'

He went down the passage and never gave Pauline another look.

Pauline finished taking off her make-up, and got dressed, and went home in perfect silence; her mouth was pressed together. Winifred thought it was because she was angry, but Nana knew it was not. She knew that Pauline was terrified to speak in case she would break down and cry. She certainly was not going to let the theatre see how much she cared, and of course she would not cry in the tube. As soon as she got into the house she raced up the stairs. She could not go into the bedroom, because the others might come in, so she went into the bathroom and locked the door, and lay down on the floor, just as she was, in a coat, gloves, and beret, and cried dreadfully. At first she cried because she thought she was being badly treated, and kept muttering, 'It's a shame; I didn't do anything.' 'Anyhow, Winifred's sure to be awful; they'll be sorry.' But by degrees, as she got more and more tired from crying, other thoughts drifted through her mind. Had she been rude? Had she been showing off? Inside she knew that she had, and she was ashamed, and though she was quite alone she turned red.

Ballet Shoes: Noel Streatfeild

Comment

This is a careful study of a twelve-year-old girl's feelings. At her audition Pauline had felt nervous and was surprised at being offered the part. Her immediate success makes her conceited not only in the theatre, as in this extract, but also at home where she expects the others to act as her servants.

The conceit, however, is not really Pauline's character, nor is losing her temper: 'She behaved as she had never behaved before.' It is interesting to note that, combined with the anger she felt at having to obey the management's rule over wearing the wrap, she felt excited; excited, that is, at the novelty and strangeness of her feelings.

Mr French makes the point, when Pauline later goes to apologize, that success usually affects people similarly. He also adds that 'it was a good thing to get that sort of thing over at twelve, instead of waiting till she was grown-up.'

Activities

— Have you ever been successful at something —not necessarily in acting? How did it affect you? Did you have to 'learn a lesson' like Pauline? Think carefully and make a few notes, prior to writing a full account.

— Find out what a call-boy did. As you may have gathered, his job was not really to carry wraps for twelve-year-old actresses!

— Pauline behaved out of her normal character. Have you ever felt that you have acted out of character, when you haven't really felt yourself, but haven't been able to do anything about it? Rather than writing down your experience as it stands, you may prefer to fictionalize it, that is, turn your experience into a story as if it were about someone else.

— Even very experienced actors and actresses refer to stage nerves while waiting in the wings before a performance. Have you taken part in a play or concert and felt like this?

— 'Fossil' is a curious surname. There is an intriguing reason for such a name; you will discover the answer in Chapter Two of *Ballet Shoes.*

Nuts and bolts

Spelling

In Unit 17 we mentioned one way in which words change when additions are made at the end. Another change: words like 'begin', 'run' and 'prefer' double their last letter when an addition is made: 'beginning', 'running', 'preferring'. This doubling only occurs when the last syllable is stressed, as if it needs strengthening to take the weight. Say our three examples aloud, and you will see what we mean. To make quite sure, add 'ed' on to each of these words, and say them aloud: propel, commit, refer.

— Find in our unit a word ending with a double letter and '-ing' (like 'running'), and another with a double letter and '-ed' ending (like 'fitted').

Unit 37

Wilbur's new friends

Wilbur is a little pig who is saved from slaughter by the cleverness of a spider called Charlotte. When she dies he is very sad, but he is consoled by three of her children, who have hatched out from the sac of 514 eggs she has left behind. They float away like tiny balloons:

When he woke it was late afternoon. He looked at the egg sac. It was empty. He looked into the air. The balloonists were gone. Then he walked drearily to the doorway, where Charlotte's web used to be. He was standing there, thinking of her, when he heard a small voice.

'Salutations!' it said. 'I'm up here.'

'So am I,' said another tiny voice.

'So am I,' said a third voice. 'Three of us are staying. We like this place, and we like *you*.'

Wilbur looked up. At the top of the doorway three small webs were being constructed. On each web, working busily, was one of Charlotte's daughters.

'Can I take this to mean,' asked Wilbur, 'that you have definitely decided to live here in the barn, and that I am going to have *three* friends?'

'You can indeed,' said the spiders.

'What are your names, please?' asked Wilbur, trembling with joy.

'I'll tell you my name,' replied the first little spider, 'if you'll tell me why you are trembling.'

'I'm trembling with joy,' said Wilbur.

'Then my name is Joy,' said the first spider.

'What was my mother's middle initial?' asked the second spider.

'A,' said Wilbur.

'Then my name is Aranea,' said the spider.

'How about me?' asked the third spider. 'Will you just pick out a nice sensible name for me – something not too long, not too fancy, and not too dumb?'

Wilbur thought hard. 'Nellie?' he suggested.

'Fine, I like that very much,' said the third spider. 'You may call me Nellie.' She daintily fastened her orb-line to the next spoke of the web.

Wilbur's heart brimmed with happiness. He felt that he should make a short speech on this very important occasion.

'Joy! Nellie! Aranea!,' he began. 'Welcome to the barn. You have chosen a hallowed doorway from which to string your webs. I think it is only fair to tell you that I was devoted to your mother. I owe my very life to her. She was brilliant, beautiful, and loyal to the end. I shall always treasure her memory. To you, her daughters, I pledge my friendship, for ever and ever.'

'I pledge mine,' said Joy.

'I do, too,' said Aranea.

'And so do I,' said Nellie, who had just managed to catch a small gnat.

It was a happy day for Wilbur. And many more happy, tranquil days followed.

As time went on, and the months and years came and went, he was never without friends . . . Charlotte's children and grandchildren and great-grandchildren, year after year, lived in the doorway. Each spring there were new little spiders hatching out to take the place of the old. Most of them sailed away, on their balloons. But always two or three stayed, and set up housekeeping in the doorway.

Mr Zuckermann took fine care of Wilbur all the rest of his days, and the pig was often visited by friends and admirers, for nobody ever forgot the year of his triumph and the miracle of the web. Life in the barn was very good – night and day, winter and summer, spring and autumn, dull days and bright days. It was the best place to be, thought Wilbur, this warm delicious cellar, with the garrulous geese, the changing seasons, the heat of the sun, the passage of swallows, the nearness of rats, the sameness of sheep, the love of spiders, the smell of manure, and the glory of everything.

Wilbur never forgot Charlotte. Although he loved her children and grandchildren dearly, none of the new spiders ever quite took her place in his heart. She was in a class by herself. It is not often that someone comes along who is a true friend and a good writer. Charlotte was both.

Charlotte's Web: E.B. White

Comment

Charlotte's scheme for rescuing Wilbur is ingenious, but we will not spoil your reading of the book by giving the show away. A girl called Fern discovers what is going on in the barn (which is on a farm in America), but at first no one believes her. Charlotte's plan works, and Wilbur becomes the best-known pig in the district, so that he is kept on permanent show by his owner. There are other interesting characters among the animals, and they all get on well together.

Of course we all know that animals cannot talk in the sense that we understand talk, but do not let that stop you reading the book, which is a good one. *Charlotte's Web* is a fable: that is, a story about animals, with a message that tells us something about men and women as well. You may remember our referring to this in Unit 9, *Practice makes perfect*. We also learn from the story that there is an America different from the one we know so well, with its skyscrapers, space explorers and atomic bombs. Even our short piece shows that life on the farm is happy and peaceful and interesting.

Activities

– After Nellie has accepted her name, she fastens her orb-line. Draw a very small web to illustrate spokes and orb-lines. What is an orbital road?
– Aesop was a Greek who lived about two and a half thousand years ago. He is said to have written numerous little stories about animals, each containing a lesson for human beings. Penguin Books publish a good edition of the *Fables*. Other fables worth reading are those of the seventeenth-century French writer, La Fontaine. We also recommend 'The Butterfly who Sang' in Terry Jones's *Fairy Tales*.
– Try writing a short fable of your own. Remember to write about animals while giving a lesson to human beings.
– Find out about Robert Bruce and the spider. What lesson did he learn?
– Read *Charlotte's Web*. It is in most libraries.

Nuts and bolts

Spelling
When we add '-ly' to 'definite' there is no change: 'definitely'. But when we add '-ly' to a word ending in 'y', like dreary', we have to change that 'y' into an 'i' before adding 'ly': 'drearily'.
– Look at our unit, and find two more examples of this alteration. One begins with 'b' and the other with 'd'.

Unit 38

The king in rags

A young king came to the throne in Scotland. After a year or two of pomp and ceremony, fine foods and silks and flattery, he began to wonder how it was with the people he was ruling over. Did they eat salmon and venison too, and drink red wine, and sleep on down pillows? More important, were they truly happy?

Of course they were, said the statesmen and the courtiers – the young king ruled over a contented prosperous people.

The king was not entirely satisfied. He had seen stick-thin arms pleading at the gate of his palace. He heard one winter that there was much starvation in the north-east; the rain had rotted the barley-harvest.

But no, said the dukes, the folk were happy in spite of individual misfortunes and communal misfortunes. The king should not worry his head about such things. If there was any worrying to be done, that burden was borne by others.

Still the king was not satisfied.

One evening he sent his courtiers away. He wanted to be alone, he said. He had important things to do, and he had to do them alone.

Once the last scented nobleman was out of the chamber, the king rang a bell, and a bundle was brought in to him by an old man and laid at his feet. The king at once took off his fine silken clothes and untied the bundle and put on moleskin trousers, and a thick jacket, and a woollen hat: the kind of dress that decent workingmen wore.

Again the king rang the bell. The old man returned, and led him by a secret passage to an exit behind the high wall of the palace. There the king in his workman's clothes mingled with hundreds of other citizens, none of whom recognised him. The king as he went along was inclined to be clumsy on the steep cobbled street, because he was used to walking on carpets and parquet floors, and once or twice he jostled a passer-by. Sometimes the offended party would smile reassuringly back at him, and sometimes he was given glares and muttered curses.

He descended steep steps into a tavern, and asked for ale at a dark counter. The tavern was full of men, drinking and talking and discussing matters of interest. No attention was paid to the newcomer.

In the meantime the king was listening to the talk at the next table. He thought that drink always made folk happy and carefree, but those subjects of his were grumbling over their mugs. 'Hard times, hard times. . .'. This new tax, how could they ever afford to pay it, coming on top of that other tax the winter before, and the drop in wages? Oh yes, and the high price of bread and beef. It was all because of the wars against the

English. What good did the wars ever do to them? It was a game that the gentry played when they got tired of hawking and playing chess – that was war. But when it came to paying for the wars, then it was the common folk who had to foot the bill.

'Ah,' said an old man. 'It was aye the same. But in the olden times the king saw to it that the common folk weren't oppressed. Ay, the king was aye a friend and a father to his folk. The king kept the nobles and the knights in their place.'

'But the present king,' said another drinker, 'he's hardly more than a boy. They keep him cloistered there in the palace. What does he know about the troubles and angers of his people?'

The king leaned over the counter and told the landlord to give all of his customers a mug of his very best ale. He left more than sufficient money on the counter. Then he went out into the light.

He knocked seven times on a blank wall.

The old man was waiting behind the secret door. He opened. Together – the old man in front, bearing a candle – they returned to the throne-room. Then the king stripped off his common clothes and resumed his silk.

The old man carried the bundle away.

The king sat down on his throne and rang another bell. Singly, and in groups, his courtiers returned from their girl-friends, their claret and apples, their games of chess. One of them stifled a yawn; there was still a long evening of lutes and dancing and jokes before midnight and his majesty's bedtime.

'Gentlemen,' said the king in an angry voice, 'all is not well with our country!'

The Two Fiddlers: George Mackay Brown

Comment

This tale comes from the Orkney Isles, islands rich in exciting stories and legends. As Norse was the language spoken there until five hundred years ago, it is not surprising that the stories bear a likeness to the Norse sagas, still very much part of the lives of the Icelanders. In the long dark winter nights, the imagination, as yet untainted by electronic entertainment, invented stories of power and simplicity, stories about ordinary people, good and bad, kings and queens, magic and mystery.

The extract we have presented is the beginning of the story, as the young king sets out to acquaint himself with life in his kingdom. His conscience, troubled by the sight of thin beggars, is not eased

by those courtiers enjoying the luxuries that obtain in the palace. He dresses, in turn, as a seaman, apprentice weaver, baker, beggar, farm-worker – and he falls in love with Inga, the farmer's daughter.

The king in disguise, trying to determine the truth about life in his kingdom in order to be a better ruler, occurs in many traditional stories. The Duke, in Shakespeare's *Measure for Measure*, adopts the disguise of a friar, the hood of the monk's habit providing a useful means of concealing his familiar face, as he fears his nineteen-year rule has become somewhat lax.

Activities

– We have deliberately withheld the ending. How do you think the story ends? Write your own ending, then compare it with the original. (There is an inexpensive edition of the book – which contains ten stories – published by Pan Books in their 'Piccolo' series.)
– Write down what the king learnt from the ordinary people in the tavern.
– Design and/or make a disguise for yourself. Would you dare go out in it and buy something at a shop, perhaps where you are well known? If you do so, record your experience. Has it helped in your understanding of the king in the tale? (You could always use your disguise at a fancy-dress party!)
– Do you think it is easier now than it was long ago, for a ruler to find out about the lives of the people? How?
– Write a story that centres on a disguise. It does not have to involve a ruler.

Nuts and bolts

Commas

One of the many useful jobs done by commas is to separate a number of things mentioned, such as items in a list.
– Look at the paragraph beginning 'Once the last scented nobleman . . .' – about a third of the way through the piece – and note the way in which the 'trousers', the 'jacket' and the 'hat' are separated.
– Then look at the second paragraph of Comment, and find there an example of commas put between items in a list.

Unit 39

Friends and relatives

As for the usual female visitors, they seemed to enjoy nothing but worries and grievances, which they poured forth on Mother. Sitting in a little chair in the corner I used to amuse myself by listening to the funny sounds of the voices, high or low, now whining, now nervously giggling, but I cannot remember ever to have heard a woman visitor laugh. Sometimes I counted the number of times they said 'yes'. One visitor was grand at this, for every now and again she would let forth a chromatic scale of the word 'yes', starting on a high note and rushing down in a torrent of concession. Some visitors would make no attempt to talk at all unless Mother kept hard at it. One day, in the middle of a deadly pause, I broke in brightly with:

'I know what you are thinking, Mother.'

Snatching at any straw, Mother was unwise enough to invite me to tell.

'You are thinking up what you can possibly say next.'

Startled, Mother looked anxiously at the visitor, who fortunately was too stupid to notice anything odd in my remark.

While acquaintances were few, we were richly endowed with relations, mostly cousins and aunts, whose notion of a visit involved far more than a mere hour's chat. Aunt Polly was the worst. We knew her knock, which became a signal for the boys to stampede to the study and become deep in their work. Exceedingly fat and affectionate, she would envelop me in her embrace, and burst into fulsome flattery as to how I was 'getting on', a 'fine girl', and 'so like dear Helen' (an aunt even fatter than herself). What annoyed Mother most was her habit of turning up about ten minutes before a meal, with loud declarations that she couldn't stop, had only just popped in, and must be off at once. When the meal had been delayed in accordance with this idea, she would catch a savoury smell and rearrange her mind. (As Tom used to remark: 'No lady smells roast chicken.') She would think that perhaps the meal would give her a chance to see the dear boys. After that it seemed abrupt to go, and she would stay to tea, and then wait till my father came home, to see dear Tom. It often ended in his having to take her home, or worse still in her being put up for the night.

Another aunt, of very different calibre, also lived within visiting range. Instead of flattering the family, she found fault. Her hobbies were correct behaviour and religion. . .

She lost no opportunity of improving our morals and manners at table, feeling that poor Mary was very lax with those boys. They, needless to say, enjoyed shocking her with their adventure stories, coloured for her benefit. During one period, she markedly left behind a little magazine, containing 'a list of persons for whom our prayers are requested'. Charles, always on the quest for the ridiculous, seized the list hopefully, and hooted with delight when he found: 'For a family of four boys and one girl. That they may be led to give up their frivolous mode of life.'

'That's us,' he shouted, and we all crowded round to see ourselves in print, but not in the spirit that Aunt Lizzie had intended.

Another distasteful point about this aunt was her regular visit once a week to give Charles and me music lessons. No child of today would believe the long hours we spent practising. I had to hold my hand so flat that a penny would not fall off, and then hammer down finger after finger on the piano. What misery the third finger gave me!

Then followed scales and more exercises, and last of all a little 'piece' which I loathed most of all. The only thing I really enjoyed was the chromatic scale, walking down the piano, and playing every note, as fast as I could.

In spite of the fun that we made of Aunt Lizzie we were really fond of her, because she never gushed and would do anything for us. And we all knew her tragedy. She had run away to be married, and her husband had turned out a drunken brute with no redeeming attraction. He tortured her to such an extent that she was obliged to flee from lodging to lodging to avoid

him, and to make a living for herself by giving music lessons. It is no wonder that she took gloomy views of life, and had such vivid ideas of hell. Victorian times are supposed to have been so settled and happy and care-free, but my recollections hardly tally with this rosy picture. Surely today no woman would endure such humiliation year after year. But then, of course, Lizzie's extreme piety may have driven her husband to drink and extreme measures.

A London Family between the Wars: M.V. Hughes

Comment

When you come to think about it, relatives are important to us all. They are responsible for our existence; they look after us while we are too young to manage for ourselves; they see us started in life; and if difficult days come, we can usually rely on them for advice and assistance. In the same way it is likely that one day we shall ourselves be regarded as sources of support in time of trouble. Most of us would like to be thought of as individuals to whom people can readily turn for help and sympathy.

It is not quite the same with friends, though a close friend can be as good as a relative. What differences do you see between friends and relatives?

Activities

– Try saying 'yes' in a number of different ways:
  – to express complete agreement.
  – agreement but with some doubt.
  – yes, of course that's obvious.
  – I suppose so.
  – do you *really* mean it?
  – I sympathize very much.

– Describe a relative or relatives whom you will remember for a long time. What do you find particularly memorable about them? You don't have to restrict it to aunts!
– Aunt Polly clearly liked to come to see the family and used any excuse to delay her departure. Can you think of reasons why this might be? What kind of life do you think she led? When you have thought about her, make up an episode not necessarily involving the family referred to here.

– 'They seemed to enjoy nothing but worries and grievances.' Do you know many people who always seem to have something to complain about, the sort of people who put a damper on everything? Note some ways of making grumblers more cheerful.
– Imagine Aunt Lizzie and Aunt Polly talking about the author of the extract. What might they have said? You can either write it as a series of notes or you can make up a conversation.
– Do you have a favourite aunt or uncle whom you could question about his or her childhood? If so, write down a few questions to help you with your conversation.

Nuts and bolts

Conversation

Towards the end of the first paragraph, the writer says, 'Some visitors would make no attempt to talk at all unless Mother kept hard at it.'

Conversation needs somebody to talk and somebody to listen. This may sound rather obvious, but have you noticed how many people do all the talking, not allowing anyone else to get a word in edgeways? And some, of course, as here 'make no attempt to talk at all'! A good conversation must involve sharing the talking and the listening.

When you have a conversation, try to listen carefully to what the other person is saying. There are many people who don't do this; these people are in too much hurry to add what they want to say to be bothered to listen to others.
– Think back to the conversation you had in the last activity or, if you haven't yet done it, think about another conversation arising from a previous unit. Did you listen carefully or were you too concerned to ask your next question?

Unit 40

Cooking our food

Before fire had been discovered, man ate his food raw. He hunted what he could and many people must have died through lack of the essential vitamins. It is believed that the burning of livestock in forest fires first gave man the idea of making fires to cook his food. When he was able to make use of fire, man probably just tossed a carcass in to the middle of a fire and hauled it out when it was partly cooked. It is likely that many years passed before some prehistoric cook thought of skewering the meat and holding it over the flames.

In many primitive parts of the world ancient practices in cookery are still carried on. Although some civilisations had discovered how to preserve meat by drying and salting, it was the people of the eastern Mediterranean countries who studied food preparation as an art. The Greeks and Romans in particular were elaborate cooks.

Centuries passed and man ate a larger variety of foods, still cooked on open fires. People on the continent of Europe were eating cooked vegetables in the Middle Ages, while in Britain the pleasures of the table consisted of meat, pastry and sweetmeats. Medieval kitchens were very large and at banqueting time many cooks were employed. Cookshops were also in use at this time. They sold hot dishes or cooked customers' own food. Not until the 16th century did anyone seriously begin to plan kitchen aids.

The existence of vitamins in food was not established until 1912. This discovery was made by Sir Frederick Gowland Hopkins who demonstrated the presence of vitamins in milk. After this, studies of food and its value to man continued and we are now aware of the amounts of each type of food needed to keep the body healthy. In the western world today it is rare for people to fall sick through lack of an essential food. Nevertheless, there is a world shortage of food and in less fortunate countries the people are grossly underfed.

Although most people do eat better food and are able to cook it on modern cookers, styles of cooking vary enormously. Food can be cooked by boiling, frying, grilling and roasting.

The British are fond of boiled meats and traditional steak and kidney pies and puddings, and stews. The Americans are renowned for their enormous steaks which are either fried or grilled, and in both countries roast joints of meat are popular. The French are also great beef-eaters. They cook it very lightly by frying or grilling, and garnish it with the most delicious sauces. They also use a great deal of butter in cooking. The Italians love pasta and eat it in all shapes and forms, while the Spanish like to eat *paella* (a mixture of shellfish, chicken and rice), and cook their food in oil.

In Europe today there is a great interchange of recipes and it is not unusual for the people in one country to cook, as a matter of course, a traditional meal of another.

In eastern countries, rice, which is either boiled or fried, is the basic dish. The Chinese accompany their rice with pork, chicken or fish, and they have their own distinctive culinary vegetables which are always very finely sliced. They are masters at blending flavours together and Chinese food is enjoyed everywhere. In India rice is served with curried dishes containing spiced meats and vegetables.

Hamlyn Younger Children's Encyclopaedia

Comment

This interesting article, taken from a modern encyclopaedia, traces man's eating habits from prehistoric times through to the present day, and concludes with a brief look at some European, American and Asian characteristics.

Most of us in the western world take the preparation and cooking of food for granted, unaware of the slow process of trial and error throughout history. Apart from the development of cooking utensils, we also take for granted electricity, which has increased our versatility in cooking with such items as mixers, freezers, and microwave ovens.

Activities

– There are very few people indeed who can remember everything they read. For most of us, if we want to keep facts and details in our minds, notes are essential. Not only are notes useful as references, but taking notes makes us concentrate more fully on what we read. Re-read the first five

You're right—it was two hours at regulo three!

paragraphs in turn, and after each one, try to note down its most important point.
– Make a chart of paragraphs six and eight.

British	boiled meats steak and kidney pies and puddings stews
Americans	steaks, fried or grilled

and so on.

– Boiling an egg is very simple, but is it so simple to describe it in words? The enormous sales of cookery books show that many people rely on recipes written down, it being important, therefore, to cover each stage carefully and logically; nothing must be omitted or out of order, nor must the wrong word be used – 'boiling' and 'simmering' are not the same. (We set out the rules for this kind of writing in Unit 2, *Nuts and bolts*.) Look at one or two recipes in books or on the side of cereal packets and see whether you think they have been well written.
– Choose a favourite recipe and try to write down each stage as clearly as you can without looking at any cookery book. Then check your answer with a book or, alternatively, ask a friend to produce the dish following your written instructions!

– Find out about carbohydrates, fats, proteins, minerals, vitamins, and say why we need each group in our diet.
– From which Latin word does 'vitamin' come? What does the word mean in Latin? Can you think of other words from the same 'root' word?
– What is the connection between teflon coating on utensils to prevent food sticking and space travel?

Nuts and bolts

Paragraphs

This is a revision of Units 4 and 23.
The second paragraph ('In many . . .') of our unit is linked to the first. You will find this link in its opening sentence, which shares an idea with the ending of the paragraph before.
– Look carefully and you will see what this shared idea is.

Paragraph six ('The British . . .') has no topic sentence to tell us what it is about.
– Try to invent one.

Unit 41

The fun they had

Margie even wrote about it that night in her diary. On the page headed May 17, 2155 she wrote, 'Today Tommy found a real book!'

It was a very old book. Margie's grandfather once said that when he was a little boy *his* grandfather told him that there was a time when all stories were printed on paper.

They turned the pages, which were yellow and crinkly, and it was awfully funny to read words that stood still instead of moving the way they were supposed to – on a screen, you know. And then, when they turned back to the page before, it had the same words on it that it had had when they read it the first time.

'Gee,' said Tommy, 'what a waste. When you're through with the book, you just throw it away, I guess. Our television screen must have had a million books on it and it's good for plenty more. I wouldn't throw it away.'

'Same with mine,' said Margie. She was eleven and hadn't seen as many telebooks as Tommy had. He was thirteen.

She said, 'Where did you find it?'

'In my house.' He pointed without looking, because he was busy reading. 'In the attic.'

'What's it about?'

'School.'

Margie was scornful. 'School? What's there to write about school? I hate school.' Margie always hated school, but now she hated it more than ever. The mechanical teacher had been giving her test after test in geography and she had been doing worse and worse until her mother had sent for the County Inspector.

He was a round little man with a red face and a whole box of tools with wires and dials. He smiled at her and gave her an apple, then took the teacher apart. Margie had hoped he wouldn't know how to put it together again, but he knew all right, and after an hour or so, there it was again, large and black and ugly. The part she hated most was the slot where she had to put test papers. She always had to write them out in a punch code they made her learn when she was six years old, and the mechanical teacher calculated the mark in no time.

So she said to Tommy, 'Why would anyone write about school?'

Tommy looked at her with very superior eyes. 'Because it's not our kind of school, stupid. This is the old kind of school that they had hundreds and hundreds of years ago.' He added loftily, pronouncing the word carefully, '*Centuries* ago.'

Margie was hurt. 'Well, I don't know what kind of school they had all that time ago.' She read the book over his shoulder for a while, then said, 'Anyway, they had a teacher.'

'Sure they had a teacher, but it wasn't a *regular* teacher. It was a man.'

'A man? How could a man be a teacher?'

'Well, he just told the boys and girls things and gave them homework and asked them questions.'

'A man isn't smart enough.'

'Sure he is. My father knows as much as my teacher.'

'He can't. A man can't know as much as a teacher.'

'He knows almost as much, I betcha.'

Margie wasn't prepared to dispute that. She said, 'I wouldn't want a strange man in my house to teach me.'

Tommy screamed with laughter. 'You don't know much, Margie. The teachers didn't live in the house. They had a special building and all the kids went there.'

Margie went into the schoolroom. It was right next to her bedroom, and the mechanical teacher was on and waiting for her. It was always on at the same time every day except Saturday and Sunday, because her mother said little girls learned better if they learned at regular hours.

The screen was lit up, and it said: 'Today's arithmetic lesson is the addition of proper fractions. Please insert yesterday's homework in the proper slot.'

Margie did so with a sigh. She was thinking about the old schools they had when her grandfather's grandfather was a little boy. All the kids from the whole neighbourhood came, laughing and shouting in the schoolyard, sitting together in the schoolroom, going home together at the end of the day. They learned the same things so they could help one another on the homework and talk about it.

And the teachers were people.

The mechanical teacher was flashing on the screen: 'When we add the fractions $\frac{1}{2}$ and $\frac{1}{4}$ . . .'

Margie was thinking about how the kids must have loved it in the old days. She was thinking about the fun they had.

Earth is Room Enough: Isaac Asimov

Comment

What they learn in the school of 2155 seems to be much the same as today: geography, history, maths. They have homework, to make sure that lessons really are learned. This homework is done by making marks or punching holes, and then it can be marked mechanically, just like the answers in some examinations today. Candidates have to black out small squares or circles, which can quickly be marked by a machine. So there are some signs that Asimov's forecast is coming true.

Even in a short piece like this we learn something about the two main characters. Tommy is confident, absolutely sure he's right, rubs in the fact that he knows all the answers, and is rather conceited. Margie is quieter, more thoughtful, and readier to learn, just because she is less sure of herself.

Asimov is writing about America, as we can tell from expressions like 'regular' and 'schoolyard', where we should say 'proper' and 'playground'.

Activities

– Do you agree with Margie that some parts of school today are 'fun'? Or would you rather learn quietly at home?
– Compose a letter to Mr Asimov, telling him what you think of his story.
– Are there any subjects, or parts of subjects, in which you would prefer a mechanical teacher?

– Make a short list of the advantages that books have over telebooks.
– It is the year 2155 and a BBC interviewer wants to talk to you about your education. You tell him or her what you like and dislike. Write the transcript of your interview. You can set it out as a script; refresh your memory by looking again at Unit 6.

Nuts and bolts

Quotation marks

We have had a first look at these in Unit 15. In the second sentence of the unit above we have an example of the way in which quotation marks go outside everything quoted, including punctuation: 'Today Tommy found a real book!'
– Look next at paragraph four, and notice what happens when Tommy's words are split by *said Tommy*. A comma is placed after the break and then the quotation marks start again with 'what a waste . . . .'.
– Two-thirds of the way through the unit the brother and sister talk together without any indication of who is speaking. How do you know when one stops and the other starts?

Unit 42

Night Mail

Travelling Post Office, Belfast station, 1935

I

This is the Night Mail crossing the Border,
Bringing the cheque and the postal order,

Letters for the rich, letters for the poor,
The shop at the corner, the girl next door.

Pulling up Beattock, a steady climb:
The gradient's against her, but she's on time.

Past cotton-grass and moorland boulder,
Shovelling white steam over her shoulder,

Snorting noisily, she passes
Silent miles of wind-bent grasses.

Birds turn their heads as she approaches,
Stare from bushes at her blank-faced coaches.

Sheep-dogs cannot turn her course;
They slumber on with paws across.

In the farm she passes no one wakes,
But a jug in a bedroom gently shakes.

II

Dawn freshens. Her climb is done.
Down towards Glasgow she descends,
Towards the steam tugs yelping down a glade of
    cranes,
Towards the fields of apparatus, the furnaces
Set on the dark plain like gigantic chessmen.
All Scotland waits for her:
In dark glens, beside pale-green lochs,
Men long for news.

III

Letters of thanks, letters from banks,
Letters of joy from girl and boy,
Receipted bills and invitations
To inspect new stock or to visit relations,
And applications for situations,
And timid lovers' declarations,
And gossip, gossip from all the nations,
News circumstantial, news financial,
Letters with holiday snaps to enlarge in,
Letters with faces scrawled on the margin,
Letters from uncles, cousins and aunts,
Letters to Scotland from the South of France,
Letters of condolence to Highlands and
    Lowlands,
Written on paper of every hue,

Comment

This poem was spoken during a film about the journey of a mail train from London to Scotland. Stop reading this paragraph now, and read the poem aloud – or get someone else to.

The poem itself shows how it should be read: some of it fast, some of it slowly. The pace varies according to the speed of the train. The first four lines pelt along as the train races on the level. Then at line 5 the poem slows; in Part II we cross the summit; and in Part III down we go at a rattling pace. In Part IV we have arrived while most people are still asleep.

In Part II the big cranes for loading ships look like an avenue of trees. The furnaces are tall blast furnaces for smelting iron.

The poem is about people as well as mail. Re-read the last lines of Parts II and IV.

●●

The pink, the violet, the white and the blue,
The chatty, the catty, the boring, the adoring,
The cold and official and the heart's outpouring,
Clever, stupid, short and long,
The typed and the printed and the spelt all wrong.

IV

Thousands are still asleep,
Dreaming of terrifying monsters
Or a friendly tea beside the band in Cranston's or Crawford's:
Asleep in working Glasgow, asleep in well-set Edinburgh,
Asleep in granite Aberdeen,
They continue their dreams,
But shall wake soon and hope for letters,
And none will hear the postman's knock
Without a quickening of the heart.
For who can bear to feel himself forgotten?

Night Mail: W.H. Auden

●●

Activities

– To the train crew the night journey was just a job of hard work probably without much excitement. Can you think of some other journeys that might mean a great deal to people not actually travelling, but are just a job of work to the driver/pilot/captain? Jot them down.
– Imagine you are one of the drivers of a London to Edinburgh coach or lorry. Describe how one journey was interrupted, perhaps by floods, a road subsidence, a stowaway, a passenger on the wrong coach.
– How do we know that the train is pulled by a steam locomotive?
– Choose half a dozen lines or so that you enjoy reading and learn them off by heart.
– Make a list of the mail delivered to your home during one week (or one month, if you prefer). Divide it into these categories:
    – personal
    – bills
    – circulars/adverts
    – others

You will need the co-operation of the rest of the family – you don't have to read the letters, merely know into which category they fall.
– The poem has a deliberate rhythm which resembles the train's movement. Read Wilfred Noyce's poem, 'Breathless', to see a slow rhythm used effectively, and Robert Browning's, 'How they brought the good news from Ghent to Aix', for an imitation of galloping horses.

Nuts and bolts

Apostrophes

We made a start on Apostrophes in Unit 27, and we come now to the second use. This is to show possession: children's clothes, Jane's bike, the company's property.

When an apostrophe is used with a word in the plural ending in 's' it is placed differently. Look at these carefully:

> That is the girl's locker (*only one girl*)
> These are the girls' lockers (*several girls*)
> My son's room is here (*one son*)
> My sons' room is here (*two or more sons*)

– To make sure you have the difference clear, look in our unit for a plural word ending in 's' with an apostrophe; and for two singular words ending in an apostrophe followed by 's'.

Unit 43

The tall Indian

This comes from a true account of pioneering days in America. As a small girl Laura travelled with parents and her sister Mary in a covered wagon in search of good farming land. They built another cabin, but – without knowing it – in territory reserved for Indians. So once again they had to move on. Jack is their dog, very fierce and protective:

Indians came riding on the path that passed so close to the house. They went by as though it were not there. They were thin and brown and bare. They rode their little ponies without saddle or bridle. They sat up straight on the naked ponies and did not look to right or left. But their black eyes glittered.

'I thought that trail was an old one they didn't use any more,' Pa said. 'I wouldn't have built the house so close to it if I'd known it's a highroad.'

As he spoke he looked up, and there stood an Indian. He stood in the doorway, looking at them, and they had not heard a sound.

Silently Jack jumped at the Indian. Pa caught him by the collar, just in time. The Indian hadn't moved; he stood as still as if Jack hadn't been there at all.

'How!' he said to Pa. Pa replied, 'How!' The Indian squatted down by the fire. Then Pa squatted down by the Indian, and they sat there, friendly but not saying a word.

Laura and Mary were quiet in the corner. They couldn't take their eyes from that Indian. He was so still that the beautiful eagle-feathers in his scalplock didn't stir. Only his bare chest and the leanness under his ribs moved a little to his breathing. He wore fringed leather leggings, and his moccasins were covered with beads.

Ma gave Pa and the Indian their dinners on two tin plates, and they ate silently. Then Pa gave the Indian some tobacco. They filled their pipes, and they lighted the tobacco with coals from the fire.

A while longer they all sat silent. Then the Indian rose up and went away without a sound.

'That Indian was perfectly friendly,' Pa said. 'And their camps down among the bluffs are peaceable enough. If we treat them well and watch Jack, we won't have any trouble.'

The very next morning, when Pa opened the door to go to the stable, Laura saw Jack standing in the Indian trail. He stood stiff, his back bristled, and all his teeth showed. Before him in the path the tall Indian sat on his pony.

Indian and pony were still as still. Jack was telling them plainly that he would spring if they moved. Only the eagle feathers that stood up from the Indian's scalplock were waving and spinning in the wind. When the Indian saw Pa, he lifted his gun and pointed it straight at Jack.

Laura ran to the door, but Pa was quicker. He stepped between Jack and that gun, and he reached down and grabbed Jack by the collar. He dragged Jack out of the Indian's way, and the Indian rode on, along the trail.

'That was a darned close call!' Pa said. 'Well, it's his path, an Indian trail, long before we came.'

Little House on the Prairie: Laura Ingalls Wilder

Osage Indian holding pipe-tomahawk

A geological surveyor talking with Pauite Indian during a northern Arizona survey over a hundred years ago

Comment

Many white settlers regarded the Redskins as dangerous, and tried to exterminate them. But Laura's Pa did not agree with this. He would not have settled near the trail, if he had known it was still in use; and he tells us that it was Indian long before the whites came. And the Indian was friendly, though he knew that the Palefaces had settled in Indian territory.

Activities

– Find out more about Red Indians from a reference book. Why were they called Red Indians? And did they ever wear the splendid head-dresses we see in films and pictures?
– When the white settlers went to America, they picked up words from the Indians which have since become part of English. What are: caribou, hickory, moccasins, papoose, pow-wow, tomahawk, totem, wampum, wigwam?
– Have you ever feared or disliked a person at first

sight, and later come to like him or her? You might like to write about it.
– One day a space-ship lands and aliens settle down in your garden. Describe what plans you make and what happens.
– As you have already discovered from reading Unit 1, *The bear in the way*, p 12, the Wilder family lived in a log cabin. How would you make a fireplace safe in a house made of wood? Read Chapter 9 of *Little House on the Prairie* to find out what Mr Wilder did.

Nuts and bolts

Spelling

In English the letter 'c' sometimes sounds like 'k' as in: account, America, comes, covered. In 'search' and other words we hear 'c' and 'h' combining to make a scratching sound; and in 'nice' the 'c' sounds like 's'.

In words like 'serviceable' and 'noticeable' the 'c' is followed by a silent 'e' to make sure that the 'c' sounds like 's'; the 'e' softens the 'c'.
– In the unit there is another word in which the spelling works in the way we have just described. Track it down.

Unit 44

A look at my head

Then one afternoon Mrs Williams hung up her apron behind the kitchen door, and put on a black hat, and a black coat with a fur collar, and went down to the village for a meeting, something to do with chapel. She was gone all afternoon. I thought she looked at me a bit oddly when she came back. After supper she got a bowl of hot water, and a bar of black soap, and a funny fine comb, and set them one end of the kitchen table. I thought she was going to wash the dog. I took no notice.

'Come here, boy,' she said to me.

'What do you want?' I said, looking with suspicion at her broad aproned chest, and rolled-up sleeves.

'Come here, boy. I am just going to look at your head.'

'Look at my head? What the hell do you mean!'

'No need to fly off at me. Mrs Jones, and Mrs Evans both say their evacuees had lice. Now I am just going to clean you up, see?'

I backed away from her. 'You're not going to touch me!' I said.

'I will not have lice in my house,' she declared, 'no matter who it is they are on.'

'There aren't any lice in your house,' I said, swaying between outrage and laughter. Watching us from his rocking chair by the fire, Mr Williams grinned broadly. I collected myself, and said in a normal tone, 'There are no lice in my hair, Mrs Williams, I have never had lice.'

'You just come here, boy, and let me see,' she said, marching toward me, comb in hand, soap in the other. I tipped up a chair in front of her, and backed out through the door to the yard.

Evan and David were out there, with a lantern in the dusk, rolling a three-gallon drum back to the shed. She came to the door, and called out to them to stop me, or I suppose that's what she was calling, for they ran after me. I jumped over the wall into the field, and ran across the grass. Sheep lumbered away from me, bleating, as I went. Shouting gibberish at me the two shepherds came down the slope behind me.

At the bottom of the field there was a dip – a sort of narrow concrete pool, with a little stream running alongside it. Last time I had seen it the dip had been empty and dry. When I felt the hard concrete under my feet, I jumped, expecting to land on the bank of the stream, and be over that too in another stride. But the concrete was wet, I slipped, fell, and plunged into five feet of stinking water. The stink was heavy disinfectant. It reeked. It burnt my nose and mouth. I coughed, sank again, and took another mouthful. There was no grip on the sides of the pool, and the top edge was too high for me to reach. I floundered. Coming up with the lantern David and Evan stood high above my head on dry land, and laughed like maniacs, hanging on to each other for support, and howling with laughter. Somehow I struggled to the end of the pool, and scrambled out.

I was so angry I thought I was going to murder them. I caught myself looking round for a stone, and feeling the blow in my mind's eye. When I took a grip on myself I began to shake all over.

They were very concerned. They hurried me up to the farm house, and stood me beside the fire, while they peeled off my sodden clothes. I was still possessed by fury.

'What in hell was that there for?' I asked through my teeth.

'It's for delousing sheep, see,' said Hugh, roaring with laughter again. But I didn't think it was funny.

'I'm going to bed,' I said, clutching the towel I was wrapped in.

'Mrs Jones told me there is a letter for you at the Post Office, and you have not been asking for it,' said Mrs Williams. I stopped on the bottom step.

'You mean, someone has been keeping my letters?' I demanded.

'Keeping them back? You are not in London now, boy. The postman cannot come round the whole mountain, just for one or two letters for the farms. Our letters stay at the Post Office till we fetch them.'

Well, how could I have known that?

Fireweed: Jill Paton Walsh

Comment

The events described above are told in a story of two teenagers adrift during the Blitz, when German bombers in the 1939–45 War were attacking London.

Thousands of children, some with their mothers, were 'evacuated' i.e. sent to peaceful country areas like Wales. Many evacuees found it difficult to settle down, away from friends and relatives, in the peace and quiet of the country.

Activities

— Imagine you are the boy, and have written home to ask if you can return to London. They say 'no' and then after two weeks in the country you change your mind and say you would like to stay there. You are enjoying the farm life, scrambling on the hills and getting to know the plants and animals. Write the letter.

— When the war is over and the boy grown-up and in a job, he goes back to Wales and visits Mrs Williams. She remembers him and the incident. Imagine the conversation.

— Make up another misunderstanding at the farm or another incident which surprised the evacuee.

— Have you ever gone to stay with friends or relatives, and found that you came into conflict with their ideas on how you should behave? Describe your feelings.

— Read, if possible aloud, the poem below by Clyde Clarkson at the age of 11:

Temper

Temper is a red hot hate which glows
*   inside you*
It takes over all love and boils it
*   And flows through your body like bolting*
*   lightning*
It sticks in you like knives of thunder
*   And feels as if you want to destroy*
And to make a revenge which you cannot make
*   To fight when you cannot fight*
*   And to rise against your enemies*
*   But this is the abominable that is not visible*
*   to us*
But all we can see is a stubborn way of revenge
*   That leads us astray to wander forever.*

The boy who fell into the sheep-dip must have felt like this. If you feel strongly about something, try writing a poem about it. There is no need to use rhymes; Clyde managed well without them, and much of the world's greatest poetry is rhymeless.

— A country boy or girl arrives to live in a bustling city, as the father has changed jobs. Write an imaginary diary of the first two days.

Nuts and bolts

Slanting

When you are writing something, your reader is not present. You have to think, 'Who is going to read my work?' Unless you are writing to friends or family, you will avoid *slang*, because it tends to be understood only by a particular group or by people of a certain age, *dialect* or local expressions that circulate only in the district you live in, and you will not be too chatty or matey.

Various groups of people, and most trades, professions and people of a certain age have their own special sets of words. (Nowadays these are called 'registers'.) Computer users, for example, have their language.

When the boy who describes his experience in the unit above writes home, his letter will be slanted.

— Re-read the letter you wrote for the first activity and see whether you made it appropriate for writing home.

Unit 45

The neighbours did not approve

Their father brought home two copies of Mavor's First Reader and taught them the alphabet; but just as Laura was beginning on words of one syllable, he was sent away to work on a distant job, only coming home at the week-ends. Laura, left at the 'Cat sits on the mat' stage, had then to carry her book round after her mother as she went about her housework, asking: 'Please, Mother, what does h-o-u-s-e spell?' or 'W-a-l-k, Mother, what is that?' Often when her mother was too irritated or too busy to attend to her, she would sit and gaze at a page that might as well have been printed in Hebrew for all she could make of it, frowning and poring over the print as though she could wring out the meaning by force of concentration.

After weeks of this there came a day, quite suddenly, as it seemed to her, the printed characters took on a meaning. There were still many words, even in the first pages of that simple primer, she could not decipher; but she could skip those and yet make sense of the whole. 'I'm reading! I'm reading!' she cried aloud. 'O Mother! O Edmund! I'm reading!'

There were not many books in the house, although in this respect the house was better off than its neighbours; for in addition to 'Father's books', mostly unreadable as yet, and Mother's Bible and *Pilgrim's Progress*, there were a few children's books which the Johnstones had turned out when they left the neighbourhood. So, in time, she was able to read Grimm's *Fairy Tales*, *Gulliver's Travels*, *The Daisy Chain*, and Mrs Molesworth's *Cuckoo Clock* and *Carrots*.

As she was seldom seen without an open book in her hand, it was not long before the neighbours knew she could read. They did not approve of this at all. None of their children had learned to read before they went to school, and then only under compulsion, and they thought that Laura, by doing so, had stolen a march on them. So they attacked her mother about it, her father conveniently being away. 'He'd no business to teach the child himself,' they said. 'Schools be the place for teaching, and you'll likely get wrong for him doing it when teacher finds out.' Others, more kindly disposed, said Laura was trying her eyes and begged her mother to put an end to her studies; but, as fast as one book was hidden away from her, she found another, for anything in print drew her eyes as a magnet draws steel.

Edmund did not learn to read quite so early; but when he did he learned more thoroughly. No skipping unknown words for him and guessing what they meant by the context; he mastered every page before he turned over, and his mother was more patient with his inquiries, for Edmund was her darling.

If the two children could have gone on as they were doing, and have had access to suitable books as they advanced, they would probably have learnt more than they did during their brief schooldays. But that happy time of discovery did not last. A woman, the frequent absences from school of whose child had brought the dreaded Attendance Officer to her door, informed him of the end house scandal, and he went there and threatened Laura's mother with all manner of penalties if Laura was not in school at nine o'clock the next Monday morning.

So there was to be no Oxford or Cambridge for Edmund. No school other than the National School for either. They would have to pick up what learning they could like chickens pecking for grain – a little at school, more from books, and some by dipping into the store of others. . .

That was indoors. Outside there was plenty to see and hear and learn, for the hamlet people were interesting, and almost every one of them interesting in some different way to the others, and to Laura the old people were most interesting of all, for they told her about the old times and could sing old songs and remember old customs, although they would never remember enough to satisfy her. She sometimes wished she could make the earth and stones speak and tell her about all the dead people who had trodden on them. She was fond of collecting stones of all shapes and colours, and for years played with the idea that one day she would touch a secret spring and a stone would fly open and reveal a parchment which would tell her exactly what the world was like when it was written and placed there.

There were no bought pleasures, and if there had been there was no money to pay for them; but there were the sights, sounds and scents of the different seasons; spring with fields of young wheat-blades bending in the wind as the cloud-shadows swept over them; summer with its ripening grain and its flowers and fruit and its thunderstorms, and how the thunder growled and rattled over that flat land and what boiling, sizzling downpours it brought! With August came the harvest and the fields settled down to the long winter rest, when the snow was often piled high

and frozen, so that the buried hedges could be walked over, and strange birds came for crumbs to the cottage doors and hares in search of food left their spoor round the pigsties.

Lark Rise to Candleford: Flora Thompson

Comment

This comes from Flora Thompson's account of her childhood in an Oxfordshire hamlet (small village), about a hundred years ago. Schools were very different then; classes were larger and conditions were harder. Teaching methods relied a great deal on repetition and learning by heart. She writes about herself in the third person, i.e. as if she were talking about someone else, and she calls herself Laura. It shows how well people can educate themselves, if they really want to and the right material is at hand. It also reminds us that people who educate themselves can arouse jealousy in others.

Activities

– Can you recall the moment when you realized that you could read? If so, describe it. Do you remember how you were taught to read? Was it by learning the alphabet first, like Laura, or by the so-called 'look and say' method, for example?
– Write of your success in learning something else, like swimming, perhaps, or riding a bicycle.
– What is your opinion of Laura's neighbours and their views on learning to read?
– The author says that she sometimes wished she could make the stones speak because they must have seen so much, owing to their age. If you could make stones speak about a particular time in the past, which age would you choose and which features of life would you be most interested in?
– In the last paragraph Flora Thompson describes how the countryside appealed to her. Which are your favourite aspects? And what appeals to you about town life? Jot down two short lists: one for the country, one for the town.
– Which five questions would you like to ask Flora Thompson about life when she was young?

Nuts and bolts

Apostrophes

We have now looked at the two uses of apostrophes. The first is to show that a letter has been omitted, in the shortened words that we say so much in conversation: 'It's' is short for 'It is', and 'should've' for 'should have'. The second use is to show possession: 'Diana's dog', 'customers' entrance' (more than one customer).
– Look through our unit and find one apostrophe for abbreviations (shortened forms), and another for possession.

Unit 46

This time next week

A London school has been sent into the country to avoid the danger of being bombed:

On the first morning we discovered Maggie enraptured by a shaggy and vacant bird's nest which had been hanging out of the hedgerow near the school for weeks. A bike, big as a bedstead, leaned against a bank of dying grass and autumn flowers.

'It's beautiful,' she was cooing, to no one in particular. 'See how intricate the little creatures have made their home. I *do* hope they hatched their family successfully.'

She beamed in her craggy way at the critical group of us who had gathered round her skirts. A new boy called Cabbagepants took the chain off her bicycle while we held her attention.

'We're going to have such fun, such wonderful fun,' she laughed as we started off towards the school together. 'Oh dear, the chain has come off. Never mind, we'll walk along together.

'We will really be able to study nature here,' she burbled. 'The changing seasons, the birds and the flowers and the first frosts. Oh, it will be such a happy, happy time!'

The old dear really talked like that. And the sad thing was she meant it. On that sweet autumn morning all the meanness and the hopelessness of that crammed, out-dated school at Kingston were no more, for her. She was ready for a new start. A clean, fresh effort, in the countryside she had probably pictured and longed for so many times in the yellowed classroom of a town school.

But the boys thought differently. Had she been a gorgeous young thing with a soft face and a panting voice we would, no doubt, have followed her joyfully through the countryside, glorying in nature, and listened still and stunned in the classroom. But she was not. She said beautiful things, but she was not beautiful. Life so quickly became hell for her.

She laboured hard enough, putting crosswords on the board to keep us amused, traipsing through the fields and woods on nature rambles, on which we quickly vanished over the horizon, leaving her breathless and distressed or just talking to herself. . .

Maggie tried so pathetically hard to be fair and kind. We usually came in loaded with sugarbeet off the carts, slipped them under our desks and munched them through the lessons.

She was a bit shortsighted and had not noticed this. But one day she spotted Boz chewing and

opened his desk. Her face cracked into one of her patient, boys-will-be-boys smiles. 'How interesting,' she said. 'Now, does anyone know what this is?'

As we had been eating the root for a couple of weeks we knew quite well, but we led her on.

'A marrow, Miss.'

'A turnip.'

'A toadstool.'

'No, you're quite wrong,' she beamed, happy and grateful that she had at last caught our interest. 'No, it's called a sugarbeet. . .'

The poor old doll chattered on, and to add a little excitement to the lesson she announced: 'I'm going to cut this one up so you can each have a piece and taste it. Just see how sweet it is.'

This sort of hilariously unpleasant thing happened every day, in two shifts, morning and afternoon. I was as bad as the rest. One day I was stood behind the blackboard for punishment and I poked the pegs holding the board out from behind . . . so that abruptly the blackboard descended on her foot. Everyone thought it was very funny.

Each morning she would bring one of us to the front of the class to read a passage from the Bible. . . One November day, with the rain washing the school's small windows, Maggie called me out and gave me the open Bible to recite. I read it as we had always read it, gabblingly fast, the quicker the better, and get it over with. But only so far like that.

Suddenly I knew what words were: that put together they sang like a song. I stumbled, then started again. But more slowly:

For lo, the winter is past,
The rain is over and gone;
The flowers appear on the earth;
The time of the singing of birds is come,
And the voice of the turtle is heard in our
land;
The fig tree putteth forth her green figs,
And the vines with the tender grape
Give a good smell.

When I got to the piece about 'the rain is over and gone' they all howled because it was teeming outside. But I did not look up at them. The words of Solomon's song made me ache inside and I was afraid it might show. I gave the Bible back to Maggie and, although she did not know it, and never knew it, she had taught her first and only lesson at Narborough. I knew about words, and I went on seeking them, discovering them, and wondering and delighting in their shape and beauty. For me Maggie had made a miracle.

This Time Next Week: Leslie Thomas

Comment

Leslie Thomas seems here to have gone out of his way to present himself and the other town boys in a thoroughly bad light. Maggie is made to look completely foolish and ridiculous; and we get the impression that there was constant war between them. But could it all have been quite as bad as this?

Activities

– Would you rather be in Maggie's class or the one we read about in *Teachers for a month* (Unit 34)?

– How do you think Leslie Thomas behaved for the rest of that day? Imagine his thoughts that evening as he turns over in his mind the words that have had such a powerful effect on him. You could make it a diary entry, perhaps.

– Re-read the words that impressed Leslie Thomas so much. Use them as a starting-point for a short description of spring.

– Would it be a good idea to arrange for town schools to spend a term in the country, and *vice versa*?

– Use your dictionary to find the meaning in this passage of: enraptured, intricate, critical, hilariously, gabblingly.

Nuts and bolts

Summaries

Try your skill some time at summarizing a news item on radio or television, without making notes. The memory can be a very useful sieve for holding the items that need to be remembered. But if you make notes on a broadcast, it is always possible to miss something important while you are writing.

– Read through our piece again, and make a note or two on Maggie's character; and then write a short summary, saying what sort of person she was.

– Then without any re-reading say what the country people must have thought about the behaviour of these town boys.

Unit 47

Children may be wiser than their elders

Easter fell early that year, while people were still going about in sledges. Snow lay on many of the roofs, or else, melting in streamlets, ran through the streets. A large pool which had oozed from the slush lay across the roadway between two cottages. It attracted two little girls, one a very little child and the other somewhat older, from these cottages. The two little girls had been dressed by their mothers in brand-new frocks; the smaller child was in blue and the elder in yellow with an embroidered pattern, and each had a smart red handkerchief fastened about her head. After they had finished their dinner, the two had run out to play beside the pool and to show each other their fine new clothes.

Then, of course, they wanted to paddle across the dirty water. The smaller one went down to the edge of the pool in her dainty shoes, but her companion cried, 'Don't go in like that, Malasha; your mother will scold you. Take off your shoes first, and I will take off mine, too.' So they both took off their shoes, and began to wade across the pool from opposite sides.

Malasha was soon in over her ankles, and she cried, 'I am afraid; it is so deep.'

'Oh no, it's quite safe,' said Akulka. 'It is no deeper in the middle. Come right across to me.'

They drew nearer to one another, and Akulka said, 'Be careful, Malasha, you are splashing too much. Do walk more gently.'

But she had hardly said this when Malasha's little foot gave a great stamp, which splashed Akulka's pretty frock all over. Akulka lost her temper and flew at Malasha. Thoroughly frightened, Malasha fled for the shelter of her home.

Just at this moment, Akulka's mother passed this way, and saw her child's frock muddied from neck to knee. 'How did you get yourself so dirty, you bad child?' she cried.

'Malasha splashed me,' was the reply. 'She did it on purpose.'

The infuriated mother chased Malasha, caught her and spanked her hard. The child's cries, ringing through the street, made her own mother come running. She began to scold the other woman, saying, 'How dare you hit my child?'

Soon the two of them were engaged in a hearty duet of abuse, and the peasants all down the street came out of their houses, the men all growling and the women all shrilling, and no one taking any notice of what his neighbour was saying. Curses and oaths soon showed signs of turning into blows, and there was a danger of a real fight breaking out, when an old woman, the grandmother of Akulka, came on the scene.

'Come, come, my good people,' she said, 'this is too bad. This is no way to spend Easter. We should all be giving thanks to God, not sinning together like this.' But the people took no notice. . . She would never have succeeded in calming them down had it not been for the two little girls themselves. While the noisy quarrel was still going on, Akulka had dried and wiped her frock and had come out again to the pool. Then she picked up a little stone and began to dig out earth and throw it into the pool so as to divert the water into the main street. Malasha also came out and started to help her by digging a small channel with a chip of wood. And still the peasants argued and disputed, while the water escaped through the tiny ditch the girls had made and ran down to the feet of the angry people and the old woman who was trying to pacify them. The happy children were running along, one on each side of the little watercourse they had made.

'Stop it, Malasha, do stop it,' Akulka cried as well as she could for laughing. But Malasha was unable to reply for her own happy laughter.

Thus the two children danced along beside their rivulet, delighted with the chip of wood which was bobbing down its rapids; and so they danced straight into the middle of the crowd.

As soon as she saw this, the old woman raised her voice again. 'Have you no fear of God, that you quarrel so miserably? Here you are all angry and disputing about these two little ones, yet they have forgotten it long ago, and are happily playing together again. Are they not wiser than you?'

Now silent, the peasants looked at the two laughing children and felt ashamed of their anger and dissension. Then laughing at their own folly, they separated and went home to their several cottages.

'Unless you become as little children, you shall not enter into the Kingdom of Heaven.'

Children may be Wiser than their Elders:
L. Tolstoy

Peasants weaving baskets in Russia at the end of the nineteenth century

Comment

The title of this Russian story gives us a hint: it contains a lesson. But people do not like reading just lessons, so Tolstoy makes it a convincing tale about two girls and a granny and a crowd, and slips in the lesson near the end. The quotation that ends the piece comes from the New Testament (St Matthew's Gospel, 18:3) and makes it quite clear what Tolstoy is aiming at, but the point is made before we reach the end. The adults are senseless and very stupid; it is the children who enjoy life, behave sensibly and have no time for senseless and stupid quarrels. Perhaps Tolstoy wrote his fable because he saw that the lesson would always be needed.

Activities

– What is the lesson Tolstoy is trying to teach? (A one-sentence answer should be enough.)
– Would things have been different if Akulka's mother had tried to find out whether the splashing really was intentional? Say very briefly what you think.
– How should Akulka's mother have dealt with a very trying situation?
– Make up a modern story to illustrate Tolstoy's lesson.
– A great many films and books contain a 'moral' or lesson buried in them. Was there one in anything you have read or seen on television lately? If so, describe it.
– A story with a moral that you would probably enjoy is *The Well-Off Kid* by Bill Naughton, from his collection of stories called *The Goalkeeper's Revenge*.

Nuts and bolts

Spelling

There is a useful jingle which nearly always decides the right way to spell a group of words in which it is easy to go wrong. 'Piece' and 'deceive' are both spelled right, though one has 'ie' and the other 'ei'. Here is the rhyme:

> *I before E*
> *(except after C)*
> *when the sound is EE.*

When you apply the rule, think first if the sound is EE. So 'i' comes before 'e' in: belief, field, thief. 'C' makes the difference in: ceiling, deceive, receive. Note that the 'c' comes *immediately* before; in 'achieve', for example, you will see that another letter comes between the 'c' and the 'ie'.

Words like 'reign' and 'weigh' do not come into it, because they have not got the EE sound. There are a few exceptions, but we are leaving them till later.
– Look through the unit and find one 'ie' word, and one 'ei' word. Does our rule apply to them?

Unit 48

The thrill of the circus

The lights dim, the band strikes up a fanfare, and the ring, thirteen metres in diameter, is suddenly ablaze with spotlights. The ringmaster in dazzling red coat announces the grand procession: first, the elephants lumber across the centre of the ring, followed by the flying-trapeze artistes in costumes sparkling with sequins. Around the perimeter of the ring come the clowns engaging the audience in conversation – or at least, trying to – one clown sporting in his lapel a large flower which shoots a jet of water into the face of another clown who comes to sniff the 'fragrant' bloom. The circus has started.

The circus provides entertainment for the family, both young and old. And as the entertainment is visual, no language barrier prevents enjoyment and the big circuses can employ artistes from several countries.

The world of ancient Greece, Rome, and Egypt had circuses with acrobats, tumblers, and jugglers similar to those of today, but the violent and bloody scenes involving wild animals and gladiators are a far cry from the modern circus.

Philip Astley, a sergeant-major in the dragoons, is really the father of the modern circus in Europe, Russia, and America. It is he who, in front of audiences in London in the second half of the eighteenth century, performed astonishing feats on horseback. His fame spread and he gradually added acrobats, clowns, and a tight-rope walker to the proceedings. So flourishing did his shows become that he was invited to perform with his company in front of Marie-Antoinette and the Court in France. Hughes, one of Astley's company and later a rival, took a group to Russia where Catherine the Great had an arena specially made for him in the royal palace. And it was one of Hughes's *protégés*, Bill Ricketts, who founded a circus in America.

Tricks on horseback, similar to those of Astley, still provide an important part of the modern circus. Horses are carefully chosen for their colour, shape, and grace of movement, so that they are pleasing to the eye. With horses, and indeed with all the many types of animals that are found in circuses, it is their intelligence and skill that amaze us, not only of animals like horses,

dogs, and chimpanzees, but also of the ferocious and potentially lethal lions, tigers, and bears. But then is it really so surprising? In order to survive in their natural habitat, the animals need to use their intelligence and skill.

All circus acts, whether with or without animals, require careful practice to reach the perfection necessary to perform in public. Acrobats straining their muscles or contorting their bodies to achieve what, to most of us, appears impossible with such ease and agility have dedicated themselves to their acts. We do not know how many times they have failed while practising. Turning a somersault having been launched from a spring-board and landing on top of a human pyramid three-people high is not learnt overnight. Nor indeed is juggling with several hoops, balls, or plates.

The drum-roll that announces the flying trapeze heightens the audience's tension; no one can witness the breath-taking leaps through space without feeling some measure of fear for the participants. The trapeze, which requires split-second timing and nerve, as well as skill, was invented by the Frenchman, Léotard, after whom the one-piece costume known as the leotard is named. He saw ventilator cords hanging from the roof of his father's swimming-pool and experimented, tying bars of wood to the cords. Failure, of course, meant getting wet!

After the excitement and fear of the flying-trapeze it is the clown who brings us safely back to earth, literally, by making us laugh. Not only does he relieve the tension, but he fills the gaps between acts, so that the ring-hands can clear away equipment used in a previous act and prepare for the next. But this is not to belittle the clowns, for they have important and skilful acts of their own. Clowns have a long history and are popular with audiences. Distinguished very often by their baggy, colourful clothes, big boots, and their grotesque make-up, they reveal a mixture of craftiness and stupidity at the same time; for the clown who is clever enough to deliver a custard-pie accurately to someone's face usually ends up being drenched by a bucket of whitewash himself!

Comment

This article hints at the range of activities that go to make up a performance at a circus. Success depends on having variety and pace, so that the audience's interest and attention are not allowed to flag. It cannot be easy to stage-manage and control the large numbers of animals, performers, and technicians involved.

Though the circus has several roots in the ancient world, it is only in the last two hundred years that the modern idea of the circus has evolved throughout the world.

Notice the way in which this article is constructed, each paragraph concentrating in the main on one aspect. The first paragraph serves as an introduction to catch the 'flavour' of the circus.

Activities

—If you have been to the circus, which type of act is your favourite? Do you like being scared—at seeing tigers perform alongside their trainers, for example? Or do you prefer to be laughing at the clowns? Jot down some thoughts.
—Imagine you are a trapeze artiste climbing the ladder to begin your act. The spotlights whirl about you and there is silence from the audience. Describe your performance and how you feel.
—Try to find out more about Philip Astley and his contribution to the modern circus. To begin with, look at a large encyclopaedia.
—A day in a clown's life. You could write as a notebook or journal entry what you think a clown's day might be like.
—Clowns are sometimes known as 'joeys' after Joseph Grimaldi. Was he in fact a circus clown? Each year, incidentally, a group of clowns gather at Holy Trinity Church, Dalston, London, to remember Grimaldi.
—Walter Macken's moving story, *The Lion*, is about a circus lion, Samson, who has a thoroughly miserable life in captivity. A young boy, Tim, decides to undo the steel bolt of Samson's cage to let him enjoy some freedom. You will find the story in *Winters Tales*.

Nuts and bolts

Note-making

If you are writing notes for your own use, it does not matter a great deal how you set them out and express them. You will use your own home-made abbreviations; there need not be any punctuation; spelling will not be so important. Though it is just as well to get the spelling right. Once you have made a spelling mistake, it is so easy to go on repeating it; whereas if you get a word right, the chances are that you will go on getting it right. Writing is not so important either, so long as you can read it later on. The better and clearer set out they are, however, the more useful you will find them.
—Make brief notes on the third and fourth paragraphs of the article

9

...ds with the station master

One day the children's father leaves home and does not return. So aided by Aunt Emma they have to move from their comfortable house in the suburbs to an inconvenient country cottage, where their mother writes stories for a living. They are poor; and one day Peter and his sisters, Bobbie and Phyllis take some coal from the station dump. Peter calls it 'mining'. The Station Master catches them and makes them realize it is stealing:

They were now able to go out in all sorts of weather such as they would never have been allowed to go out in when they lived in their villa house. This was Aunt Emma's doing, and the children felt more and more that they had not been quite fair to the unattractive aunt, when they found out how useful were the long gaiters and waterproof coats that they laughed at her for buying for them.

Mother, all this time, was very busy with her writing. She used to send off a good many long blue envelopes with stories in them – and large envelopes of different sizes and colours used to come to her. Sometimes she would sigh when she opened them and say:

'Another story come home to roost. Oh, dear! Oh, dear!' and then the children would be very sorry. But sometimes she would wave the envelope in the air and say:

'Hooray, hooray. Here's a sensible Editor. He's taken my story and this is the proof of it.'

At first the children thought 'the proof' meant the letter the sensible Editor had written, but they presently got to know that the proof was long slips of paper with the story printed on them.

Whenever an Editor was sensible there were buns for tea.

One day Peter was going down to the village to get buns to celebrate the sensibleness of the Editor of the *Children's Globe*, when he met the Station Master.

Peter felt very uncomfortable, for he had now had time to think over the affair of the coal-mine. He did not like to say 'Good morning' to the Station Master, as you usually do to anyone you meet on a lonely road, because he had a hot feeling which spread even to his ears, that the Station Master might not care to speak to a person who had stolen coals. 'Stolen' is a nasty word, but Peter felt it was the right one. So he looked down and said nothing.

It was the Station Master who said 'Good morning' as he passed by. And Peter answered 'Good morning.' Then he thought: 'Perhaps he doesn't know who I am by daylight, or he wouldn't be so polite.'

And he did not like the feeling which thinking this gave him. And then before he knew what he was going to do, he ran after the Station Master, who stopped when he heard Peter's hasty boots crunching the road, and coming up with him very breathless and with his ears now quite magenta-coloured, he said:

'I don't want you to be polite to me if you don't know me when you see me.'

'Eh?' said the Station Master.

'I thought perhaps you didn't know it was me that took the coals,' Peter went on, 'when you said "Good morning'.' But it was, and I'm sorry. There.'

'Why,' said the Station Master, 'I wasn't thinking anything at all about the precious coals. Let bygones be bygones. And where were you off to in such a hurry?'

'I'm going to buy buns for tea,' said Peter.

'I thought you were all so poor,' said the Station Master.

'So we are,' said Peter confidentially, 'but we always have three-pennyworth of halfpennies for tea whenever Mother sells a story or a poem or anything.'

'Oh,' said the Station Master, 'so your Mother writes stories, does she?'

'The beautifulest you ever read,' said Peter.

'You ought to be very proud to have such a clever Mother.'

'Yes,' said Peter, 'but she used to play with us more before she had to be so clever.'

'Well,' said the Station Master, 'I must be getting along. You give us a look in at the Station whenever you feel so inclined. And as to coals, it's a word that – well – oh, no, we never mention it, eh?'

'Thank you,' said Peter. 'I'm very glad it's all straightened out between us.' And he went on across the canal bridge to the village to get the buns, feeling more comfortable in his mind than he had since the hand of the Station Master had fastened on his collar that night among the coals.

The Railway Children: Edith Nesbit

Comment

The family was very hard up and they all felt the cold in bad weather. Peter tried to help his mother by stealing railway coal, disguising the real nature of his action by pretending that he was a miner. The Station Master took a lenient view of the theft without glossing it over, and showed himself – as in this passage – a kindly and generous man who never used his position of authority to bully the wrongdoers. The children for their part were unhappy about what they did, and were glad to have the incident forgotten. To them the railway was the source of much lively interest and happiness, for their mother was so busy earning a living that she had not enough time to look after them.

Even this short incident shows us what sort of people both the Station Master and Peter were.

Activities

– These words could describe Peter's feelings when he met the Station Master: depressed, unhappy, embarrassed, dismayed, upset, disturbed, guilty, displeased, confused. Which two do you think best sum up what he felt?

– Describe any event in your life that made you feel guilty afterwards. If you like, you can turn your account into a short story using a different name for yourself.

– Mention some thoughts that must have passed through the Station Master's head after he caught the children stealing coal and found out why they did so.

– Write Peter's diary entry for the day he made friends with the Station Master.

– Later in the story the children avert a train smash by promptly reporting a landslip on the line. It is a gripping account. Try reading the book, which has been very popular and was made into a film.

Nuts and bolts

Note-making

When you are writing notes for other people to read, abbreviations will have to be reduced, and be intelligible; writing and spelling will have to be good.

– Make notes on today's six o'clock news for someone who does not get home in time to hear them. (See Unit 31 for an example of a full, well-arranged note. You will find our method of setting out the notes, complete with headings, a useful one.)

– Try a note of a different kind on the stages by which Peter moves from fear of the Station Master to friendship with him. You will need about four sentences on separate lines.

Unit 50

Pegasus – the winged horse

Bellerophon has been asked by the King of Argos to find and destroy the Chimera, a fierce monster with a lion's head, the body of a shaggy goat, and a dragon's tail. It breathed fire and moved very fast. Rex Warner, in *Men and Gods*, takes up the story:

Bellerophon knew the difficulties and dangers of his task, but he gladly and willingly undertook it. His courage however would not have proved enough if he had not been helped by the goddess Minerva.

She told him that he could never conquer the Chimera without the help of Pegasus, the winged horse who had sprung to life from the blood of Medusa, whom Perseus slew. He now lived on Mount Helicon with the Muses, never yet having felt the weight of a man upon his back. So Bellerophon set out once more on a long journey. He found the horse, a wonderful and swift animal, snow-white and smooth as silk not only over all his skin but also where the gleaming white feathery wings lay along his shoulders. For a whole day Bellerophon tried to throw a bridle round the animal's neck, but Pegasus would never allow him to come close enough to do so. Whenever Bellerophon approached, the horse would either gallop away out of reach or would rise on wings in the air, alighting farther off in the cool meadows where he grazed. In the evening, worn out and despairing, Bellerophon lay down to sleep. He dreamed that Minerva had come to him and given him a golden bridle. On waking up he found that this was actually what had happened. At his side was a beautiful bridle of gold and with this in his hand he immediately set out to look for Pegasus. When the horse saw the bridle, he bowed his head and came gently forward, willingly allowing Bellerophon to bridle and mount him. Then he sprang into the air and sped like a shooting star through the clouds to the country where the Chimera lived; for the horse was a divine horse, knowing exactly for what reason he was wanted.

Flying over the deep gullies and rocky caves in the mountains, Bellerophon saw beneath him the red glow of fire and smoke ascending into the air. He checked the course of Pegasus and flew nearer to the earth, and soon appeared the vast body of the monster as it came raging out of its lair. Pegasus hovered over it as a hawk hovers above its prey, and first Bellerophon shot his arrows into the great goat-like body below him, until the ground was drenched in blood. Then he swooped down through the clouds of smoke, thrusting his sword over and over again into the animal's neck and flanks. It was not long before the Chimera lay dead and sprawling on the ground. Then Bellerophon cut off its head and said goodbye to the noble horse who had helped him, since Minerva had told him that once his task was accomplished, he must let the animal go. Pegasus was never again mounted by any mortal man. He sped away like lightning. Some say that he went back to the grassy pastures of Helicon and that where his hoof struck the ground there issued forth the fountain of Hippocrene. Others say that it was at this time that Jupiter set the winged horse among the stars.

Men and Gods: Rex Warner

The War God's horse song

I am the Turquoise Woman's son.
On top of Belted Mountain
Beautiful horses – slim like a weasel!
My horse has a hoof like striped agate;
His fetlock is like a fine eagle plume,
His legs are like quick lightning.
My horse's body is like an eagle-plumed arrow;
My horse has a tail like a trailing black cloud.
The Little Holy Wind blows through his hair.
His mane is made of short rainbows.
My horse's ears are made of round corn.
My horse's eyes are made of big stars.
My horse's head is made of mixed waters
(From the holy waters – he never knows thirst.)
My horse's teeth are made of white shell.

The long rainbow is in his mouth for a bridle.
   And with it I guide him.
When my horse neighs, different-coloured sheep follow.
When my horse neighs, different-coloured horses follow.
   I am wealthy, because of him.

   Before me peaceful,
   Behind me peaceful,
   Under me peaceful,
   Over me peaceful –
Peaceful voice when he neighs.
I am everlasting and peaceful.
I stand for my horse.

The War God's Horse Song: Navajo Indian

Comment

Here we have a story of 3000 years ago and an old Mexican Indian poem. When stories and poems last a long time it is usually a sign that there is truth in them. In this case the truth is the enormous value the horse has been to civilized man for thousands of years, enabling him to move about his world and live by agriculture. In fourteenth-century England a trained war-horse, fit for a knight, cost nearly a hundred pounds – the life-time's earnings of a labourer. In your grandparents' time (1950) there were still 300 000 horses working on English farms; now there are only 3000.

   Both story and poem show the pleasure and pride that owners used to take in their horses. The first piece is about god-like creatures and the second is put into the mouth of a god, but both writers sound like men describing splendid animals they actually knew.

Activities

– Ask the Librarian where you can find Rex Warner's *Men and Gods* and *Greeks and Trojans*. Try some modern stories about horses such as K.M. Peyton's *Flambard* series; note that they appeal to boys as well as girls.

– Another story tells how Bellerophon tried to fly Pegasus to heaven, but the horse refused and threw his rider. Write the story – about a page in length.
– Nowadays we rarely believe in dangerous monsters (though remember Unit 11 about the Loch Ness Monster), but there are still opportunities for men and women to show courage and resource in meeting modern perils and problems. Think of some. Perhaps you could write a modern myth.
– Write a poem about a fine horse, or a short story, perhaps about one neglected, and then brought back to health by a young owner.
– Look up Horses in an encyclopaedia, and note down six points for a two-minute talk on 'Horses and people as partners'.

Nuts and bolts

Capital letters

– Look at the first eleven lines of the unit, and note all the capital letters. Decide what they are there for, and then jot down the rule for using them. Remember to keep the rule in all your own writing.

Books recommended

Unit

1 Laura Ingalls Wilder — *Little House in the Big Woods*

2 Brian Glanville — *Goalkeepers are Different*

4 Nicholas Fisk — *Robot Revolt*
Ted Hughes — *The Iron Man*

5 Alan Ayckbourn — *Ernie's Incredible Illucinations*

7 Charles Kingsley — *The Water Babies*
William Blake — 'The Chimney Sweeper' (two poems)

8 Gerald Durrell — *The Drunken Forest*
D.H. Lawrence — 'Snake'
Alan Wykes — *Snake Man*

9 Richard Adams — *Watership Down*
Kenneth Allsop — *Nature Lit Their Star*
Richard Bach — *Jonathan Livingston Seagull*

10 Marjorie Dark — *Comeback*

11 A. Conan Doyle — *The Lost World*

13 John Christopher — *Fireball*
The Guardians

14 Charles Dickens — *A Christmas Carol*
Dylan Thomas — *A Child's Christmas in Wales* (also in *Quite Early One Morning*)

15 Nicholas Fisk — *Space Hostages*

16 Jack London — *Call of the Wild*
White Fang
To Build a Fire

19 Geoffrey Trease — *Under Black Banner*

20 Leon Garfield — *Devil-in-the-Fog*

21 Joan Aiken — *Midnight is a Place*

22 Robert Westall — *The Watch House*

24 William Mayne — *Pig in the Middle*

25 Bernard Ashley — *All My Men*

26 Rosemary Sutcliff — *Dragon Slayer – the story of Beowulf*
Dawn Wind

27 P. Fitzgerald — *Jock of the Bushveld*
Grey Owl — *Sajo and her Beaver People*
R. Guillot — *Kpo the Leopard*

M.K. Rawlings — *The Yearling*

29 Ian Serraillier — *The Silver Sword*
Anne Holm — *I am David*

30 Charles Dickens — *Great Expectations*

31 Richard Adams — *Watership Down*
William Cowper — 'Epitaph on a Hare' (together with his account of tame hares) may be found in
Geoffrey Summerfield — *Voices I*

32 Mark Twain — *Huckleberry Finn*
Life on the Mississippi
The Prince and the Pauper
Tom Sawyer

34 William Mayne — *No More School*
Ray Jenkins — *The Whole Truth*

35 Charles Dickens — *Nicholas Nickleby*
Hard Times (early chapters)

36 Noel Streatfeild — *Ballet Shoes*
Curtain Up

37 E.B. White — *Charlotte's Web*
Aesop — *Fables*
Terry Jones — *Fairy Tales*

38 George Mackay Brown — *The Two Fiddlers*

39 Roald Dahl — *George's Wonderful Medicine*

40 Helen Cresswell — *The Pie Makers*
Norman Lindsay — *The Magic Pudding*

41 Peter Dickinson — *Heartsease*

42 Robert Browning — 'How they Brought the Good News from Ghent to Aix'
Wilfred Noyce — 'Breathless'

43 Laura Ingalls Wilder — *Little House on the Prairie*
The Long Winter
A.R. van der Loeff — *Children on the Oregon Trail*

44 Jill Paton Walsh — *Fireweed*
Nina Bawden — *Carrie's War*

46 Leslie Thomas — *This Time Next Week*

47 Bill Naughton — *The Goalkeeper's Revenge*

48 William Macken — *The Lion*
Noel Streatfeild — *The Circus is Coming*

49 Edith Nesbit — *The Railway Children*

50 K.M. Peyton — *Flambards*
Rex Warner — *Greeks and Trojans*
Men and Gods

Index

The references are to the numbers of the units.
C means 'Comment', and **NB** means 'Nuts and bolts'. **A** stands for 'Activity'; and the number after **A** tells us which activity. Thus 7 **A**3 directs us to the third activity in the seventh unit; and 23 **A**5 points to the fifth activity in the twenty-third unit.